ROOMS

DESIGN
AND
DECORATION

ROOMS

DESIGN
AND
DECORATION

JOHN STEFANIDIS

TEXT BY

MARY HENDERSON

DESIGNED BY

PAUL BOWDEN

PHOENIX ILLUSTRATED

First published in 1988 by George Weidenfeld & Nicolson Ltd

This paperback edition first published in 1997 by Phoenix Illustrated
Orion Publishing Group, Orion House
5, Upper St. Martin's Lane
London WC2H 9EA

British Library Cataloguing-in-Publication Data
A catalogue record for this book is available from
the British Library

ISBN 1-85799-926-6

Filmset by Keyspools, Golborne, Lancashire
Colour separations by Newsele Litho Ltd
Printed in Italy by Printers Srl, Trento
Bound by L.E.G.O., Vicenza

Frontispiece:
The print room at Netherton

Page 6:
A kitchen at Patmos

To all the people whose kind forbearance
has allowed me to create the rooms that
make this book.

John Stefanini

CONTENTS

INTRODUCTION

Rooms, like people, have different faces – wear different clothes. Some hide under heavy make-up, others wear none; some choose fashionable colours, others prefer classical simplicity. Some rooms project a fantasy image of their owners, others give a true picture of the owner's character and way of life. Early historical documents and books on design and decoration tell us about the structure of people's houses and rooms, and also give us an insight into their lives. But are these paintings, sketches and plans accurate? Is this what the artist saw or is it his romantic interpretation? We will never know. But such questions are not relevant today for, with modern photography, as in this book (even though a photograph tends to

John Stefanidis in his Chelsea studio

the room; chairs were there to be drawn up, not to line a wall. Symmetry was abandoned – asymmetry was the fashion. Rooms began to be furnished according to their function: for entertaining, for family life or for reading and study. Throughout Europe the trend was quickly followed.

In Britain the Victorian era of clutter and cover – where everything seemed to be covered in heavy, deep red-braided velvet or plush – gave way to the antithesis, to William Morris, to Bloomsbury austerity, to Modernism and Post-Modernism. Although the social changes created by the French Revolution and Britain's Industrial Revolution irrevocably altered the course of design and decoration, it is wrong to fix dates or make

flatten out a room and anchor furniture, losing mobility and the fluctuation of light), a contemporary style is registered. There are no imaginary embellishments, no cheating, the record is clear.

Over the years fashion and social change have dictated the pattern of how rooms have been arranged, altered and rearranged. Each fashionable look, first avidly copied, then overdone, was later checked and reversed. In the seventeenth century, for instance, design was a man's prerogative, the architect was the main creator of rooms, and in keeping with his plans furniture was usually lined up against the panelled walls and set out in rigid fashion. Later, in the eighteenth century, ladies and their upholsterers intervened and the scene changed. Walls were lined with fabric – often to the architect's disgust as it camouflaged his work – fabric was used for bed hangings, draped over doors, made into ample curtains and used for upholstery. And all materials in a room were often in a matching pattern and colour, giving a unified green look, or blue look, or gold and white impression. Gradually this phase changed when architects took the lead again, designing their own furniture and working with a team – usually a decorator and an upholsterer. The French Empire architects Percier and Fontaine were among the first in this field in the nineteenth century. Furniture became mobile, was moved around, placed at right angles to the fireplace, or in the centre of

sweeping generalizations on styles and their evolution because styles move in cycles and rarely full circle. They often repeat themselves but turn up in a new guise having – sometimes even unconsciously – assimilated national and contemporary influences. Today it is hard to find a label for the 1980s, as a battle is raging – a free-for-all tussle of styles and criss-cross influences. Perhaps this is due to our jet-age culture where a plethora of ideas, colours and forms from all over the globe is speedily picked up and disseminated on TV, in movies and in the press, bringing taste and style, once the prerogatives of a chosen few, within everyone's reach.

In the past most of the historical data on style and trends came from plans and inventories of important buildings, stately homes and palaces, because these kept more accurate records. Now, although stately homes, palaces and period buildings are being restored, it is the ever growing number of houses, factories, offices and apartments that have to be designed and decorated. A designer like John Stefanidis must therefore have flexibility, for he can be called to renovate a fishing lodge, a small *pied-à-terre*, a derelict mews house or stable, a modern apartment, a castle or a stately home. These could be anywhere in the world – Britain, France, Greece, the USA or the Middle East, all places he has worked in. For this task Stefanidis' art stems from a wide knowledge and appreciation of past masters coupled with an eye that has culled detail and beauty from his extensive journeys – which include South America, the countries of the Middle East and, most important of them all, India. When working on a project he can choose, enhance, revive or reject traditional patterns, interpret and also sometimes copy designs he has met on his travels. As a true artist he can create out of these influences a style that is his own, that is contemporary, harmonious, elegant and pleasing. It is restrained and original, but it has a firm classical base. It combines the rules of structure with a variety of decoration carefully chosen to suit a building, a room, an era – and a person, the client. In 1898 Tolstoy defined Art as 'an activity by means of which one man, having experienced a feeling, intentionally transmits it to others' (Leo Tolstoy, *What is Art*). Stefanidis clearly does this, but Tolstoy goes further and adds that 'the recipient of a truly artistic impression is so united to the artist that he feels as if the work were his own and not someone else's'; and this maxim for a successful designer's relationship with his client has always been John Stefanidis' aim.

Childhood and early years

Early influences are important – indirectly and subconsciously they leave a mark. John Stefanidis was born in Cairo in 1937. His Greek parents, who stemmed from Corfu, were Alexandrines, their families having lived in that ancient, teeming Middle Eastern city with its rich mixture of colour, race and traditions for three generations.

French, considered at that time the most prestigious European language, was initially planned to be John's mother tongue so his parents sent him to a French *lycée* kindergarten. But after a brief period his father moved to Eritrea to join the British Military Mission (set up in 1941 after the Abyssianian campaign) and John was sent first to a Greek Orthodox church school and then to a small, hastily assembled English school where his British education began.

John's recollections of those very early years – from the age of four – include exciting trips in Dakotas and seaplanes back and forth from Cairo and stops at Khartoum where the family stayed in a large hotel conveniently next door to the zoo. Visions of Asmara are still vivid in his mind. The clean mountain air, the rainy seasons followed by brilliant sunshine; the handsome Copts in their cotton or woollen gowns; the women with long plaited tresses, the men in flowing robes clutching their tall staffs There was fun too (and wit and gaiety are often found in John's work), as his favourite form of transport was riding in a *calessino* – a buggy for two harnessed to a prancing horse left behind by the retreating Italians – driven by the flamboyant former Italian riding master in a cock-feathered hat. Other recollections are of his parents' house on the port of Massawa. This was a huge trellis cube which, by filtering the air, always kept the temperatures cool. Later that trellising was to inspire his furniture and screens (*pp.49,155*) and he has longed for it to replace the draughts and noise of modern air-conditioning devices.

After the war John's father remained in Eritrea, where he bought salt and potash mines, and in order to continue his son's education he sent him to Egypt in the care of an uncle and aunt. After three years of preparatory schooling which John wryly remembers as mainly being taught the joys of dancing round the maypole, he moved to the English School in Heliopolis. There the curriculum for the cosmopolitan, multiracial students dispensed with prayers for Moslems and Jews to the envy of the Christians, but included English and European history, a snatch of Arab history and Bible classes which John found came to life vividly as the Bedouin, riding in from the desert, tethered their camels outside the school windows. But throughout the period from 1952, when the monarchy was overthrown, to 1954 when Colonel Nasser became President, Cairo was in tumult and the school was often closed. Frequently a cordon of soldiers had to protect the school as rumours circulated about some parents who had been imprisoned or placed under house arrest while others had risen to power. Despite the upheavals John remembers his schooldays as being happy, with pleasant holidays when he sped to Alexandria sitting in a red velvet train compartment, or was driven through the desert at break-neck speed where he saw more mirages than there could possibly have been. Thus fantasy and imagination had played their early part; the desert's infinite space and Alexandria's mixture of hedonism and art were to leave a lasting imprint.

For recreation his high-minded uncle took him – or 'dragged' him as he recalls – to the Cairo Museum instead of the movies. But twenty years later, when he came back to the museum on his way to India, he found he knew every corner – where every statue was to be found. Thinking back John finds it hard to judge how much he was influenced by this passion for Egyptology but he admits that the light – gold in Cairo and pearl in Alexandria – had a great influence on his work and this is evident throughout this book.

John returned to Eritrea during the long summer holidays but, at the age of fifteen, he travelled to Greece for the first time. Here he was struck by the clear piercing Attic light that dazzlingly rebounds off marble temples and whitewashed walls, and the softer purple evening veil – so different, he recalls from the tomb-like severity and one-dimensionalism of Egypt.

Oxford followed. After 'spending ten days in London on the way and going to twelve plays' he sat his Oxford entrance examination. John had visited Oxford in the past but did not know Brasenose, which was to be his college, and looking around he was deeply depressed by the gloom, the dripping walls and the winter darkness. He prayed he would fail the test but in fact he passed and his Oxford years were crammed with gaiety. His 'unheated rooms' looked over the Radcliffe Camera (by James Gibbs) and All Souls (by Nicholas Hawksmoor) – early inspirations for a budding designer .

When he came down from Oxford, he worked for a time for the advertising agency CPV (Coleman, Prentice and Varley). But after a year, when his work permit ran out, he was forced to go abroad and he joined CPV's newly-opened branch in Milan. There his job was administrative and he learnt about deadlines, discipline, efficiency and how to delegate – experiences that were to serve him well in the future. In Italy at that time there was what was called 'Il boom' and Milan was its centre. The town was bursting with talent as artists and writers, Romans, Florentines and Neapolitans, jostled for jobs and fame. There is no doubt that Italy influenced John's decision to become a designer. Its infinite variety of architecture, colours, paintings, frescoes and bravura are clearly reflected in his work.

A period in Greece followed and, still uncertain of what he wanted to do, he tried his hand at real estate. This was not a success. In Athens he

1. *Op art sculpture in a bedroom with painted walls.*

2. *Stefanidis-designed unit and chrome sculptures in a music room.*

delighted in his roof-top apartment overlooking the Parthenon but he found his compatriots in business tricky. He left, having bought a plot of land, and travelled all over Greece, then a country untouched by tourism.

First commissions in London

By 1967 his mind was made up – he had decided that he wanted to work and live in London. Although he had had no formal art training John knew he could design. He had already renovated some houses on Patmos and designed the interior of a yacht which he describes as 'all chrome, steel and formica, very comfortable, clean lines, pale cream and buff colours and very restful'. Brimful of new ideas and styles he first decorated his own house in London which, when pictures were published in *Queen* magazine, attracted considerable attention (*Fig. 1*), and he worked on friends' houses. He was also commissioned to decorate a lakeside house in Geneva where his novel treatment of abstract shapes confusing the perimeters of the hall was immediately picked up by *Connaissance des Arts*.

Among John's early contracts was a music room for Christopher Blackwell of Island Records in Kensington. The room had to be dark so he painted it chocolate brown. Inspired by Vasarely he added huge floor cushions to give colour. He also designed his first pieces of furniture for this room – large, slick lacquer and chrome cabinets – a design he has repeated to this day, changing the surfaces, using or discarding the chrome (*Fig. 2*). Another project was 'Joldwynds' in Surrey, a 1930s house built by Oliver Hill, the architect and designer whose later work embraced Modernism and Art Deco (*Fig. 4*). John responded readily to its style, given both his affection and respect for Art Deco – elements of which are often to be found in his rooms today alongside his contemporary or traditional furniture. 'Art Deco', he believes, 'was much more revolutionary than Art Nouveau and immensely innovative'.

Allowing free range to his capacity for fantasy and wit, John also designed two balls. One in 1969 for Viscountess Lambton in her 1930s London house built by Freda Casa Mores, was decorated with swirling colours and a gold and silver floor; the other, in 1970 for Mrs Paul Channon, was even more sensational, and had a two-storey-high tent, Kabuki designs and platforms at different levels. The tent was lined in varying shades of pink and the ceiling hung with clusters of white balloons which reflected the graded shades of pink. There were giant paper flags with camellias *en relief*, and strings of ping-pong balls as curtains with electric lights in them.

Style and international projects

Parallel to his work in London, John began restoring more houses on Patmos. Although he has now renovated some ten houses on the island and set a style for others to follow, he feels that restoration is a less valid artistic expression than building anew. 'The rustic idiom in design', he argues, 'is the assimilation of the local vernacular architecture in detail and materials. In restoration contemporary methods of building and materials are used without being evident – so restoration is really a form of artifice.' He has only built one house from scratch on the island, for the German publisher Axel Springer (*p. 112*), and hankers for more.

The centre of his international design operation today is the John Stefanidis studio in Chelsea where the doors and window surrounds are painted Mediterranean blue – a foil to London's winter grey. And as his team of twenty specialists, which includes about seven architects and highly trained assistant designers, bend over their drawing boards and his secretaries tap out detailed specifications on their word processors, the atmosphere of precision and concentration is like that of a space shuttle launch. Now that he is one of the foremost British designers, it is interesting to trace the direct influence of his early years on his work. In his style, which could be described as Modern – a counter-current to Colefax & Fowler, with a different use of colour from David Hicks – form, order and discipline have always been his masters. The use of light, for which he is so renowned, surely comes from those sharp shafts of Middle Eastern and Mediterranean sun. Even if it is dark and gloomy outside, his rooms glow with light. His windows – dressed with pull-down blinds behind bouffant balloon shades or floating unlined double curtains or even half-drawn plain straw or muslin blinds – all give the impression that they are there to keep the sun in check, and that it is just outside. His mirrors, often in pairs, his rows of plain silver 'flower pot' vases crammed with flowers (*Fig. 5*) his polished chrome, steel, brass or lacquer furniture (*p. 108*) pick up and throw out light.

Concealed lights tucked away in ceiling mouldings, or behind cupboards or shelves, illuminate his rooms too (without a single bulb showing) and enhance his carefully chosen, carefully mixed pale or bold coloured, dragged, stippled or stencilled walls. On the practical side, reading lamps – sometimes in brightly polished brass – are scattered around, and there are lights at different levels. His kitchens and bathrooms are always functional as well as splendidly luxurious.

When approaching a new project, John first takes in the street and the exterior of the building, because he believes that when decorating you 'must look out of the window'. The scene outside is always carefully interpreted and reflected in his work. Then he studies his client's way of life and surveying the rooms with a laser-beam eye, he decides whether to conserve, alter or gut. But the most crucial moment comes when he discusses the work with his client: when he tries to find out what he or she has in mind. What 'finish' is required – should it be a marble bathroom and specially designed fitted furniture or should it be a marbelized or tiled bathroom, practical, with less expensive fittings? Should it be silks or cottons? The question of a client's taste, aspirations and ambitions is vital too. There are those who hate stripes that others love; those who cannot bear certain colours and rule out, say, green or blue, or superstitious clients who think that bird designs or feathers are unlucky and furniture with animals' feet is unsavoury. Some people cling to totally unsuitable but beloved objects, while others do not really know what they want. John's role is to guide, help and interpret – which is sometimes hard. One client, for instance, sent him a tape of *Dynasty* and wanted her home to look like Joan Collins's apartment. But at meetings she felt sick – taking decisions was too much of a strain. Another client wished to meticulously restore a derelict Palladian villa on the outskirts of Athens. Looking back rather sadly on this project, John feels that 'although historians have agreed that restoration is in part invention', the careful copies of antique borders, mouldings and floors and all the architectural details were carried out very successfully according to his brief. Yet when work was completed the client's wife

3. Venini glass and Stefanidis furniture in a Kensington bedroom.

4. The sitting room at 'Joldwynds', a 1930s house by Oliver Hill.

preferred the rose-covered cottage she had moved into during renovation. The task of a successful designer is to generate harmony and to instil confidence so that a client can express his or her own style, which the designer must then bring out in his work, adding his own interpretation, expertise and design. John's aim is to do this and evidence that he often succeeds is best spelt out by a recent client, the owner of a prestigious eighteenth-century stately home. Her words: 'There are many talented interior designers but to my mind John is the only one with the flair of genius, he is in a class of his own. He does not seek to thrust his personality on the client nor the house or room or whatever it may be. He prises out with perfection what is there and transforms it into something of great beauty and originality.'

The contemporary designer's role

Fashion can be said to be a form of mimicry. A style is created by a designer – then quickly copied and commercialized. The danger is that in this rapid process beauty often suffers. Things are not necessarily 'desired because they are beautiful but found beautiful because they are desired' – an idea put forward in Paris as early as 1801 (C. Percier and P. F. L. Fontaine, *Recueil de décorations intérieures*). Since we live in an era of Designer and Interior Decoration explosion – fired by the influences and products of giants such as Terence Conran and Laura Ashley – do we need interior designers? Now that so many windows display festoon blinds – easily obtained from leading stores and by mail order – and most housewives have tried their hand at papering, painting, stippling or stencilling? Now that almost all magazines and decorating shops offer to bring swatches, wallpaper and trimmings to your doorstep, what is the need? 'Do-it-yourself' decorators can produce a fashionable, quick and effective cover but this often lacks the understanding of architecture and of scale, the attention to detail, quality, craftsmanship and finish. John Stefanidis' trained eye strips a room or house to the bare bones. Building work and the creation of harmonious space precedes all decoration. Ceilings are raised or lowered, partition walls removed or added. All this creates new volumes and restores shapes to mutilated rooms. Finally, when a project has been completed, John and his team proudly claim it will be trouble-free for many years.

Contract procedure

In his design studio, this is how John works. Stage one is a meeting with a potential client on site or at the John Stefanidis studio where they run through, and establish, procedure, time schedules and fees. Further meetings with the client are then arranged, perhaps three or four, again in Stefanidis' studio and on site in order to gauge the concept, the requirements, the practicalities, budget comparisons and the evaluation of personalities – really to find out what the client likes: what finishes; what to incorporate in the way of pictures, furniture, etc; what kind of kitchen is required; what bathrooms and fittings; what areas and special requirements are needed for children, staff, etc.; and any such points as hi-fi cupboards, paint finishes, the use of wood, marble, mirrors, etc. These meetings are attended by the senior architect, the design expert in charge of fabrics, and an administrator and co-ordinator.

A survey follows and accurate measurements are taken; surveys and

5. John Stefanidis' house in Cheyne Walk.

6. Neo-classical interior in a London mews house.

reports that are made for the purchase of a house are, in John's opinion, rarely accurate enough. After these are completed, he holds an internal meeting with the senior architect, assistant architect or draughtsman and other experts depending on what architectural changes and innovations are necessary, and the general character that is to be given to the project. As most of the work is the conversion of existing houses there are often problems which would not arise if the buildings were new and designed by him. Internal meetings are held to discuss the 'brief', plans drawn up, changed and approved and made final for the architectural presentation to be submitted to the client.

In the meantime, meetings are held in the studio to discuss furnishings. These lead to the 'Furnishing presentation' – the presentation of sketches of rooms, colour boards of paint samples and fabric swatches, samples of wood, marble, mirrors, trimmings and whatever else is needed for the job. Also furniture drawings and suggestions. When the presentation is accepted a budget is drawn up, unless a budget has been previously set to which all the plans adhere.

Working parallel to this procedure, the architects draw up their working drawings and specifications, which take some two to three months. Once the building contract starts, supervision lasts between three months and three years depending on its size. Orders are placed for all the joinery items not included in the building contract and the fabrics, carpets, etc., so that they will be on hand in time for final completion of the contract. Once the contractor is out of the building, specialist painters – if required – and carpets and soft furnishings are moved in.

This is but a sketch of the operation – a disciplined procedure where John, who is a perfectionist, takes all final decisions but allows his teams working on projects maximum independence. At meetings he sits and listens to their interpretation of his client's needs; he approves or disapproves of their suggestions, he points out the flaws or enthusiastically adopts their ideas. This teamwork is an enmeshed contribution of ideas, but always firmly marked by John's ordered style. He is good at delegating, encouraging the talent of others, increasing their confidence, and by being a catalyst he stimulates new ideas and solutions. As a result a number of members of his teams have now established their own practice after working with him.

The final look of John Stefanidis' rooms may be conventional or unconventional, yet they will all have a contemporary cloak – perhaps barely visible. There will always be harmony, comfort, restraint and a respect for the architectural character of the building, and in particular for the requirements of those who are to use the rooms he designs. For his clients John can open a Pandora's box of colour and design: colours such as those he picked up from the piles of powder outside Indian temples which inspired his first fabrics; designs influenced by painters such as Bronzino, Carpaccio or Veronese; shapes and designs based on intensive research or furniture he has seen on his travels. Not unlike the British aristocrats of the eighteenth century who returned from their Grand Tours laden with items for their collections, Stefanidis returns from his journeys with a myriad of techniques, objects and ideas for his rooms and houses.

'Getting it right' is his forte and his aim. This means getting the 'right' backcloth and making the 'right' arrangement and choice of furniture for his client's rooms. In Fig. 1 the painted wall which confuses the eye as it masks the contours of an ordinary room is the right backcloth for the movement of the Soto sculpture and the Oldenburg-style soft sculpture encompassing the TV. Fig. 2 is an exercise in arrangement with an excellent grenadine backcloth and also shows Stefanidis' first furniture design. It is a simple piece carried out in lacquer and chrome. Fig. 3 shows more furniture designs by Stefanidis in good plain, bright colours – shades of pink and yellow. The Corbusier chair is wittily covered in velvet. Often small and inexpensive details give the right atmosphere, as in Fig. 5 where the rococo exuberance of the white porcelain chandelier is well matched by the lavish group of Stefanidis flowers. This is then played down by his utilitarian flower table – inspired by an illustration of a humble room taken from Mario Praz's *History of Interior Decoration*. The design for the cupboard in the background was adapted by Stefanidis from a design by Borromini.

Enlivening what Stefanidis calls 'conventional and inevitably predictable spaces' can be seen in his work in the 1960s and 1970s, for example, the Eaton Square bedroom (*p. 141*), and more dramatically in Pimlico where Stefanidis used variations of brown throughout until suddenly on the top floor there is a brilliant mural on a white background (*Fig. 1*). The insides of concealed cupboards were painted bright green or red, the bathroom a vibrant yellow.

Originally renowned for his modern design, Stefanidis can now be said to edit any style he chooses and improve upon existing architecture. There is a beautiful example of a 1980s neo-classical adaptation in a mews house which he has reconstructed (*Fig. 6*). It is restful – the pale colours engender this; there is comfort with traditional Edwardian easy chairs and a Stefanidis sofa with low arms to give a feeling of more space. There are lacquer tables, a large stone-topped sofa table, neo-classical heads and prints which are repeated throughout the house. The carpet, a combination of traditional and contemporary design, was made for Stefanidis, as were the unostentatious fireplace and the neo-classical mirror above it. Throughout the room Stefanidis has displayed clean lines, symmetry and simplicity – almost as if the room had been chiselled out of marble.

It is the extensive variety of his work – from marble swimming pools to palaces, cottages and yachts – that partly accounts for his importance, coupled with his ability to maintain a strong thread of noble design, of form and structure – punctuated here and there with a witty flourish of bravura, as in his stencilled walls, his 'window' stars in the ceiling of an indoor pool, and his columns, mirrors and console tables with their giant Ionian volutes.

This book covers two decades of Stefanidis' design and decoration. The first part illustrates whole projects, where rooms in a building are linked harmoniously although they are treated individually. The second part illustrates rooms which serve the same purpose – such as bedrooms, sitting rooms, bathrooms and kitchens – but each one designed in a different manner to suit their use, the client's taste, the period of the building and the climate. Talleyrand has written that 'the embroidery of life is elegance' – and this is what John provides masterfully. His rooms are elegant, they have no gimmicks, no nostalgia. He is even able to create elegance in a cowshed (*p. 145*) and this he has done in his country home in Dorset.

HOUSES
AND
APARTMENTS

FORT BELVEDERE

A duke's folly, a king's banqueting hall, a grace-and-favour residence and finally – and perhaps never to be forgotten – the scene of the dramatic abdication of a young king for the woman he loved passionately: such is the history that envelops the romantic tower as it lies perched up on a hill six miles from Windsor Castle.

The 'Building at Shrub's Hill', or the Belvedere as the original triangular structure with its hexagonal crenellated towers on each corner was called, was built as a summer house in 1755 by Isaac Ware for the Duke of Cumberland (1721–65), George II's third son. It was first mentioned in 1757 by Mrs Delany (Mary Granville) who, after a merry picnic on the Duke's Mandarin yacht, which in keeping with the taste of the time was in Chinese style and 'gay as gilding and japanning can make it', went on a sightseeing tour of the 'Tower on Shrub Hill'. (Japanning was a term used for the imitation of lacquer.) Mary Granville's voluminous correspondence vividly records society life in the eighteenth century and her description, confirmed in the 1765 Royal Inventory, talks of the tower's hexagonal Great Hall up a winding staircase (probably now the main bedroom and called the Queen's bedroom after Wyatville's extension for George IV, pp. 24–6) where the predominant colour was blue; the windows hung with blue festooned blinds (in the inventory, 'window curtains'); the carved mahogany sofas; the stools and squabs covered in blue silk damask. In the centre of what may have been a domed ceiling there was 'a beautiful' Chelsea porcelain chandelier 'that cost £600'. The walls were decorated with stucco flowers and fruit picked out in colour, and blue and white china displayed in circular blue and gold shelves. The two other turrets were painted – one blue and gold and the other green; both had matching festoon blinds and carved circular bookcases

filled with leather-bound and 'gilt lettered' books – over two hundred of these – 'of different English authors'. Up the winding stone staircase there was 'a strong worsted rein line with forty brass strung loops to run it through'. (The original staircase as it is today is shown on p. 28).

Other items in the Inventory that add props to the scene at Shrub's Hill include a telescope in a mahogany case (the view from the tower was said to include Windsor Castle, St Paul's Cathedral and the Hog's Back in Surrey, which was the boundary of Windsor Park at the time), writing, card and backgammon tables, painted candlestands, yew-wood elbow Windsor chairs and painted floor cloths. Decanters, tumblers and wine carafes were housed in the butler's pantry which was 'under the stairs', while the kitchen range was fitted out with shelves and spits and the scullery with a large lead cistern and a sink lined with lead.

In 1827 Sir Jeffry Wyatville extended the tower for George IV (1762–1830), turning it into a fort. The brick exterior was coated with cement to simulate stone and the joints 'garnetted' with flint chips. Battlements were constructed and thirty-one guns, cast at the Royal Foundry between 1729 and 1749, positioned there. A bombadier, housed in the cottage which linked up with the Fort (now used as a guest house but no longer linked to the Fort), blasted a twenty-one gun salute on royal occasions and the delighted King entertained in a grand style in the newly constructed octagonal room on the north side which became his banqueting hall (this is now the drawing room, p. 21).

Wyatville and others made further additions to the original tower leaving its final shape a neo-gothic mêlée. Then, after a brief period as a grace-and-favour residence, it remained empty and neglected until 1919 when Edward Prince of Wales and his equerry Sir John Aird drove

up to the Fort. Much to Sir John's distaste, as he could see little of beauty in the 'unstately ruin … the dust was inches deep. Splintered floors, sagging doors and no more than two or three WCs in the whole establishment,' the Prince fell in love with it on the spot. 'I must have it,' the Duke said excitedly over and over again, and promptly asked his father to give it to him. The King, somewhat puzzled with what his son could do with 'the queer old place', muttered as an afterthought, 'Those damn weekends I suppose.'

From that day on, for seven years, the Fort became the Prince's, and later the young King's, 'get away from people home' as he had once called it. It was a new royal concept to say the least, but the Prince threw himself energetically into modernizing it – his equerry remarked that he showed the same enthusiasm in this task as he had shown for golf. He installed a Turkish bath in the basement (this is being resuscitated and an exercise room added), and in the grounds constructed a swimming pool (out of a lily pond) and tennis courts. He became a keen gardener and planted old-fashioned flowers – phlox, sweet williams, nasturtiums and delphiniums, as well as rhododendron bushes – and his weekend friends complained that they were bulldozed into helping him hack back the overgrown garden. Such was his love for the Fort that after his abdication he even installed door handles and hinges which he had removed from Belvedere in his mill in France, the Moulin de la Tuilerie, near Gif-sur-Yvette, Seine-et-Oise, where once again he made a garden and tried to recapture the atmosphere of an English country house.

Diana Cooper's description in her autobiography *The Light of Common Day* gives a graphic picture of life in what she called 'that Royal folly', that 'child's idea of a fort', complete with battlements, 'cannon, cannon-

continued to be as informal as always with the King often serving his guests personally. 'Frock-coats were out-moded almost by law.'

Perhaps some of these early pictures of the Fort flashed through Stefanidis's mind when he undertook the redesigning of the Belvedere's ground floor. The new owners had begun some of the decorating but quickly realized that the colours and treatment were wrong. As they did not know what to expect from Stefanidis they suggested he start on the ground floor. But very soon after this he was asked to work throughout the Fort.

The young purchasers of the Fort's coveted Crown Lease spend part of the year in Canada and when they are in England they and their teenage children fill the house with friends. Today Fort Belvedere is a romantic but practical country house where family and friends can live comfortably with all the necessary extras for indoor and outdoor fun and entertainment. Even though work remains in progress – furniture, pictures and mirrors added or eliminated, a conservatory under construction, and decoration still under way – the scene is very much as it was conceived. The rooms used for entertaining are light and restrained, the bathrooms luxurious, the bedrooms have specially-designed Stefanidis chintzes, furniture and four-poster beds. There is even an imposing closet where rackets, polo sticks and riding boots are packed in as neatly as in a trompe l'oeil picture. On a sunny day children ride over the fields towards the fairy-tale castle, while guests splash in the Prince of Wales's pool or play tennis. The Duke of Cumberland's folly, George IV's banqueting house, the Prince of Wales's toy fort, is now a family home – a Canadianman's castle. And to make dancing easier, the huge low centre lamp in the octagonal hall can be raised by pressing a button on the wall.

The inner hall

There was little architectural reconstruction needed at Fort Belvedere. It demanded instead a respect for the existing elements of the tower-structure with its mock-gothic features and for the 'modernization' carried out by the Prince of Wales in the 1920s. Today the inner octagonal hall (p. 16) sets the atmosphere of the Fort under its new owners: it has purity and style; it is uncluttered and light.

balls and the little furnishings of war'. 'The sentries, one thought, must be of tin'. Her guest bedroom on the first floor was pink all over – blinds, sheets, soap and even 'pink-and-white-maided'. The Prince's bed-sitting room was on the ground floor (now the library). The idea of a 'bed-sit' in those days, and indeed for a prince and later a king, was daringly modern – as were the chrome fittings and the black linoleum in the bathroom that led off it. (Stefanidis has retained this room unchanged. He admired the fittings but found the rest 'surprisingly unluxurious'.)

The Prince's *tenue* as recorded by Diana

Cooper was usually 'plus 20s with vivid azure socks' for golf in the daytime, and at night a Donald tartan dress-kilt 'with an immense white leather purse in front', an exquisitely fitting jacket, a costume-bonnet and a specially pleated jabot 'like John Wesley'. After dinner he played the pipes, marching round the table in the octagonal hall, and then his guests 'reeled to bed at 2 a.m.' Wallis (Mrs Simpson) was 'admirably correct and chic'. Nothing much changed when the Prince became King except that the quality of the writing paper improved – Diana Cooper had found the original paper 'disappointingly humble' – and the atmosphere

The domed ceiling, which was first given a pseudo-stone effect, has now been painted white, and the walls, which had been given a similar 'stone' treatment, have been carefully repainted in a more realistic manner to look like actual stonework. The bare boards of the original floor, which in the 1930s was covered in linoleum with a complicated star motif cut into the centre, now have a pale marble honed surface. Stefanidis had made two other suggestions for this floor – using either wood or black and white marble – but his clients wanted something lighter.

A pair of Italian seventeenth-century marble busts frame the drawing room door; one of these is thought to be of Ambrogio Spinola – the famous Genovese general who fought for Spain in the Netherlands in the seventeenth century. Stefanidis rejected a number of busts for this position – some because they were in poor condition, others because they were not the right size. It took time to find ones which look so well in their setting.

It is the central octagonal mahogany table designed by Stefanidis (he uses it again, *see p. 98*, painted in a stone colour with a marble top), together with his large lantern with real candles, that give a feeling of bold confidence: a kind of anchor to the room and even to the whole house as all the main ground-floor rooms, with the exception of the dining room, lead off it. For the centre of this table a seventeenth-century blue and white Japanese Arita plate was found, and the owners – who are polo enthusiasts – added their impressive display of trophies.

The 1930s cornice lighting has been retained but in true Stefanidis style the switches – and this includes the one that raises and lowers the central lantern – are hidden behind a movable wall panel.

The turret writing room

The turret room (*opposite*) leading off the hall is a writing room. The semi-circular desk was specially designed to fit the tower's rounded wall. It has round drum ends and brass galleries. On it there are two simple Stefanidis candlestick lights and a rare print of the Duke of Cumberland's Mandarin yacht with the original triangular tower in the background. Two seventeenth-century lidded Imari vases stand on the rounded desk ends, and on each of the two windowsills there is a *Compagnie des Indes* vase (these are a pair and were made in China for export to Europe). The central chandelier is similar to the one hanging in the second turret room (*p. 29*) just opposite the study and emphasizes a feel of continuity in design. They were specifically made for the turret rooms as it would be difficult to find a genuine pair of suitable antiques. The French-style chair, which is in fact an eighteenth-century English one, has a loose cover to match the walls and the festoon blinds which are all in Stefanidis' simple 'Esrajim Stripe'. This unobtrusive ticking stripe pattern creates the warm and enclosed feeling of a tent in this small private study.

The entrance hall

The entrance (*above*) at Fort Belvedere is not grand. It is a passage with a honed marble floor – a continuation of the inner hall's treatment.

When Stefanidis began work at the Fort in 1981 the house was virtually empty, but now the combination of lights – cornice lighting and down lighting – the repainted simulated stone walls and the furnishings set the style that greets guests arriving at this little castle. A converted bronze urn from the 1925 Paris Exhibition sheds light on a simple fabric-covered table; and an eighteenth-century gilt console table with a rust-veined marble top by William Kent, which was found for the entrance, stands beneath a decorative Elizabethan portrait of a lady in her formal garden. On either side of the table there are two antique English painted hall chairs. A large lemon tree in a Chinese pot and flowers on the table refute any impression of a fortress and emphasize that this is a country house.

The dining room

This was a characterless room when work started. To improve it Stefanidis put in an overmantel, stippled the walls a warm shade of ochre and marbelized the pilasters (*below*).

With the owners' Irish connections in mind, two eighteenth-century Irish sideboards and an Irish mahogany side-table with claw feet were chosen. Round the extendable early nineteenth-century mahogany dining table there are comfortable chairs specially designed to suit the size of the room. They have practical loose covers tied on with bows. Two splendid, large still-life paintings with marbelized frames add a feeling of substance. There is a fine collection of Chinese blue and white porcelain and a pair of these vases is held up on gilt *torchères*.

The curtains, with a full green frill, are in a Colefax and Fowler fabric; they draw, a Stefanidis requisite, although he intended them usually to be left undrawn with his Roman blinds, in 'Shades', pulled down instead. On the floor plaited straw matting is laid, a traditional covering which has been used in England since Elizabethan times.

The octagonal drawing room

There was a small Aubusson carpet in the drawing room (*opposite*) before Stefanidis started work on the house, and this gave him a clear indication of the owners' taste and choice of colours. He then had an octagonal needle-point carpet made in Portugal following the Aubusson design. The silk taffeta curtains, the colour of a pale peach, have knife-pleated edges that sit generously on the floor. In keeping with the 1930s look, which Stefanidis wanted to retain, the pelmets are plain and a sober contrast is struck by the use of simple pull-

down blinds in his white on natural 'Stripe'.

On the sofas, easy chairs and ottomans the fabrics used are small prints (mainly his 'Varese' and 'Angela') which, together with the peach curtains and the two-toned cream and white walls, add restraint to a large room. The walls had previously been painted to simulate pine panelling. This was the choice of the Prince of Wales together with Mrs Dudley Ward, a great friend who also helped him decorate York House.

Stefanidis believes that the first step in designing a room is to have a focal point – a piece of furniture of character, a beautiful mirror or an interesting picture – something that will act as a basis for the general scheme. With this in mind the first purchase for the drawing room was a set of eighteenth-century English furniture attributed to John Linnell, which consists of a sofa, two bergères, and other armchairs all painted in gold and white. To complement these, additional furniture, pictures and ornaments were found for the owners and shown to them for their approval.

Throughout the decoration they worked jointly with John Stefanidis to create the room. There is a nineteenth-century English rope stool and others like it are scattered through the house. A *Compagnie des Indes* dinner service is displayed on the shelves above the sofa which was designed by Stefanidis and covered in his 'Varese' fabric. The scatter cushions are covered in silk. Other decorative touches include a Chinese gentleman on a deer made of bronze standing on a coffee table with a fossil-marble top, an eighteenth-century Italian mirror, and eighteenth-century French and seventeenth-century Italian drawings.

As work still continues at the Fort, since these photographs were taken the mirror has been changed for a gilt one attributed to Matthias Lock, a furniture designer who interpreted the rococo in an English manner. And the pictures on either side of the arch now hang right up each side, enclosing it like an arbour. The small room that leads into the drawing room, where there is a piano, has its walls lined with important drawings. There is also

an eighteenth-century marquetry commode which is English but decorated with urns in the French manner. The huge armchairs and sofa, brass reading lamps and cornice lights, marquetry furniture, interesting drawings and decorative items make the glowing peach-coloured drawing room a comfortable and pleasant room. It is elegant without being over-formal, in spite of the disciplined layout of the chairs and ottomans, and the graceful curtains add a definite feminine touch.

A *trompe-l'oeil* chest

Not all decorating ideas are an immediate success, as the story behind this beautiful *trompe-l'oeil* chest (*detail opposite*) shows. Stefanidis decided to surprise his clients by having the chest, which was originally dark and heavy, painted in the manner of Stéphane Boudin. But alas, it turned out that this particular chest was their favourite piece of Provençal furniture. However, it is now the focal point of an attractive, well-planned bedroom. The broken plate (*below*) painted on top of the chest matches the set of china in the room.

A guest bedroom

This bedroom looks well proportioned now, but in order to achieve the effect Stefanidis had to block up a window to enable him to place the bed to best advantage.

A feeling of ease is created by the mixture of French Louis xv style furniture, the colourful Bessarabian carpet and the cotton fabrics. The sunburst pleated tester and the inner curtains of the four-poster bed are in Stefanidis' black and white dot cotton fabric 'Shades', while the outer curtains and bed valances have his crisp yellow butterfly design 'Farfalle'.

For comfort there is an easy chair and a pull-up stool designed by Stefanidis and covered in yellow. The dressing table and the bedside tables were specially made for the room – much easier and better than searching for ones that would fit. The bedside tables have white muslin skirts over a buttercup yellow chintz. Hanging over the 'flower table', with its blue and white porcelain top from Schleswig-Holstein, is a twentieth-century Venetian mirror.

The stone-coloured walls in this agreeable room, where there has been no attempt at grandeur, lead into a luxurious bathroom with ample cupboard space, white walls with a beige band, chrome fittings, a huge heated towel rail and clear strong light.

The main bedroom or Queen's bedroom

This is a grand room (*right and p. 26*) and always has been, for it must be the Great Hall which Mrs Delaney mentioned when she visited the Duke of Cumberland's folly in 1757. Now it is the main bedroom retaining some of the original cornices. The two turret rooms with seventeenth-century plaster ceilings which lead off it were transformed into bathrooms by the Prince of Wales in 1930. Stefanidis has kept this arrangement after redesigning them.

A large bed stands against the only wall where there is space for it and comes well out into the room. Mock-gothic furniture, painted grey and picked out in white, was made by Stefanidis for the room: this includes two bedside tables, half-moon commodes which cover the radiators and provide storage space, two small tables and two large cupboards with carved finials which have been placed opposite each other. The walls are painted grey with only a simple white line making it obvious that it is simulated panelling.

The coral and beige 'Fort Belvedere' fabric which adds colour to the grey and white background was designed specially for this room. It is draped sparingly over the four-poster bed to give more light; following the posts '*à la Polonaise*', it is gathered up and held at the apex by a corona. The same chintz covers the button-backed sofa, the slipper chairs and is also used for the gothic windows. These are swagged in a traditional manner but have separate linings – a treatment Stefanidis prefers as it allows curtains to fall more naturally.

The Bessarabian rug matches the tints of the room, whereas the eighteenth-century English 'sleeping' chair covered in dark green provides a bold splash of contrasting colour. A pair of small gothic open fan firescreens have been transformed into lamps with circular pleated shades. Recent additions to the room are the two gothic chairs which belonged to Horace Walpole and came from Strawberry Hill. This room which now has a gothic atmosphere and a feminine air too – appropriately since it is called the Queen's bedroom – is almost identical to Stefanidis' original concept and the presentation drawing he showed his clients before work began (*left*).

The turret bathroom

The bathroom (*right*) was left very much as it was in the 1930s. The original bath was kept and a basin installed, and in the niche there is a cupboard with a concertina magnifying mirror with a light above it in the 1930s style. The bath and basin surrounds are marble, but the walls below the dado are marbelized – softer and of course cheaper than using real marble.

The tower staircase

The tower staircase (*left*) was carpeted when Stefanidis first saw it, but he returned it to its original state: the stone was exposed and a rope and brass rings were installed. Straw matting was used to cover the stairs and the walls were sponged in a golden yellow. The same technique and colour for the walls were used to link up the staircases and corridors throughout the house. A marbelized wooden urn was specially designed to fill the niche.

The second turret

The other turret (*right*), which was only a passage when Stefanidis started work, is now used for serving drinks. Access to the kitchen was made through a mirrored door. The Russian-style chandelier is one of a pair which he made using purple glass (the other hangs in the writing room). It was the owners' idea to cover the walls with etchings and engravings with paper frames in the style of print rooms of the eighteenth century. The subjects of the prints include botany, topography of the area and polo – the owners' favourite sport.

A RIVERSIDE APARTMENT

A small and rather dingy apartment in a solid red-brick Victorian building overlooking the Thames in Chelsea is now a bright, chic London *pied à terre*. This was the result of a successful collaboration between John Stefanidis and his American client Ann Getty, after visiting the building prior to the purchase and jointly discussing its flaws and limitations. These included the bad positioning of the apartment block's pipes which made radical changes in the installation of a new kitchen and bathroom difficult, and the grim view of the entrance hall over a well with a thousand pigeon droppings. But now – the apartment having first been gutted – all is changed.

The hall

The newly-built entrance shuts off the well and light buff-painted panelled walls, discreet jib doors, pillars and bold cornices, together with a dazzling marbelized floor, give the tiny hall (*opposite*) a touch of unexpectd grandeur. A pair of Regency candelabra flanks a dashing portrait of John Smith M.P. by Pompeo Batoni, the renowned late eighteenth-century Italian portraitist who painted visiting Englishmen in Rome. The glittering painted *trompe-l'oeil* floor was inspired by the great marble floors in the Royal Palace at Caserta outside Naples. Stefanidis proposed alternatives for this floor and was delighted with Ann Getty's enthusiastic choice. When appropriate, the central heating is concealed and here it is fitted behind the hall shelf. The lanterns on either side of the jib door are a Stefanidis design, and two eighteenth-century English wooden cut-out figures put there by the owner complete the charade.

The sitting room

The only daylight in the hall, which is lit by electric light, comes through the double glass panel doors which open out into the sitting room. Although this large room has but one window, the walls – a pale putty wash gently dragged over white – and the pair of carefully placed mirrors give it luminosity and cast a golden glow. In front of the bay window overlooking the river a window seat has been fitted: it provides space to sit or lie and gaze at the river, and has an added advantage as it conceals the heating.

The festoon blinds have frivolous rosettes at the top but are played down by the use of a Stefanidis cotton fabric, 'Varese', and the simple off-white roller blinds. The squabs are also covered with 'Varese' and the different shades of hand-woven striped silks on the cushions, are offcuts found by Stefanidis in a Florentine mill. The oval-backed painted chairs, scattered round the apartment and gathered round the eighteenth-century dining table when needed, were designed for the flat because both he and Mrs Getty disliked 'brown furniture'. As is often the case in Stefanidis' interiors, both woven and printed fabrics have been used for the chairs and sofas. The soft and subtle colours of the upholstery and walls are complemented by a very large Agra carpet dotted with red flowers with an unusually wide coloured double border.

The architectural balance of this room comes from the symmetry of the bookcase, which fills the whole of one wall, and the pair of eighteenth-century German gilt mirrors with their candle sconces on either side of the bay window. The glass-fronted doors of the bookcase bring light to the windowless end of the room. The sense of formality is accentuated by the carefully placed furniture, the pairs of objects, and the many-faceted lacquered tables on which sit a pair of eighteenth-century Chinese cloisonné enamel dogs.

The original presentation sketch (*below*) has been closely followed: slight deviations include an eighteenth-century baroque lacquer commode instead of the classic *demi-lune* shown in the sketch, a drawing instead of a mirror over the commode, and different lamps. The beautiful commode (*p. 31*), the drawing by Balthus above and the objects on the commode all add to the understated elegance of the room. The Indian figures carved in ivory were bought by the owner and are placed under the gilt lamp beside the plain silver pot of flowers – both of these are Stefanidis designs.

The baby grand piano was a prerequisite, described by the owner as like 'trying to park an Oldsmobile in the living room'. Other items of furniture by Stefanidis include armchairs and a sofa, a large ottoman covered in a wool fabric – useful for extra seating or as a table, and a fretwork drinks tray on legs inspired by an eighteenth-century design. The painting by Thomas Daniel above the sofa (*c.* 1805) depicts the entrance to a temple in southern India, and the smaller picture to the left is of a Lycian tomb by Luigi Mayer.

The bedroom

Once again the presentation drawing (*left below*) for this bedroom closely resembles the finished arrangement, although the position of the bed has changed. The large, lightly stippled four-poster bed, with its domed tester and pleated inner valance, and the imposing cupboard were both designed for the room. The bed's swagged draw-up curtains, held up with tasselled rope, are a seventeenth-century treatment; at that time they were dropped to keep the bed enclosed and warm. The tester, curtains, armchairs and run-up stools are all in Stefanidis' 'Emma' fabric printed on a beige ground. The design is adapted from an eighteenth-century English woven silk in the Victoria and Albert Museum. (It has been used with a white background in a town house in Toronto, *p. 76*.) The interior of the bed is lined with Stefanidis' 'Angela', a traditional cotton stripe, and the counterpane is lightly quilted. On the floor there is a Bessarabian rug. These were originally made for the Russian market as a cheap alternative to French Aubusson carpets.

The most charming piece of furniture in the room is an eighteenth-century Russian travelling desk with a multitude of secret drawers and decorative candle sconces. The wood is a mixture of ebony and mahogany and has ormolu mounts; the small early nineteenth-century chairs are also Russian. An adjustable reading light and a spacious cupboard are the practical aspects of the furnishings of this room as is the large walk-in cupboard (not shown) of cherry-wood veneer, with its generous hanging space, shelves and drawers and well-lit full-length mirrors. Bearing in mind the owner's love of books, which already line the drawing-room walls and are scattered throughout the apartment, Stefanidis has included a simple bookcase in one of the recesses in the wall.

NETHERTON

A house, like a family, passes through a succession of births and deaths: at times it is loved and cherished, at times it grows old, flakes, disintegrates and is abandoned. Then suddenly it is loved again and garlanded with new additions. New voices echo in the rooms and new hands tend the surrounding garden. Such is the history of Netherton, a perfect grey and red brick English 'dolls' house' standing screened from the outside world behind giant rounded clipped yew hedges and rose-covered garden walls.

It was first mentioned as the rectory of the prosperous hamlet of Netherton in the parish of Faccombe in Hampshire. A survey carried out in 1618 described it thus:

> One fayre parsonage house much thereof new builded and a sellar made by Mr Andrew Reade Esq., with diverse barns and a pigeon house and certain back sides with stone walls about them made by the same Andrew Reade and an orcharde and meadow ground, thereunto adjoininge on the south side thereof.

Later, in the eighteenth century, alterations were made which included the positioning of the windows as they are today. The rector continued to live in the house until 1920, but his adjoining church, of Saxon origin, was demolished and re-erected up the hill at Faccombe where it now stands. Further additions and some demolitions (the Victorian wing was taken down) were carried out by the various owners of Netherton who bought it because they fell in love with its solemn face – there are features of the house which have been attributed to Inigo Jones – or left it because of its

silence and isolation. The topiary and many of the yew-hedged 'rooms' were created by John Charrington who bought the house in 1955. According to one story, when taking a neighbour round his garden – a rather formidable lady at that – he was heard to say 'I love yew'! John Charrington also made several architectural changes and extended the library on the south side following careful plans by the architect Raymond Erith.

As work was being carried out on the extension a large, very early cylindrical tank, beautifully enclosed in narrow bricks, was discovered; its purpose at the time must have been to store water drained from the roof. Only eight cottages remain of the original hamlet but extensive excavations have been carried out by the City of London Archaeolog-

ical Society (John Charrington was its former President) together with the British Museum where some of the eighth-century objects which were discovered are now exhibited.

Stefanidis has often worked on houses with an interesting history and his approach always combines reverence to historical and architectural detail with his client's taste and requirements. He does not enforce his own style and ideas but rather adjusts them to the particular project. Netherton cannot be described as a great house historically, but it is an interesting building. Today Stefanidis' stencilled walls are an excellent background for the owners' important collection of pictures; the bedrooms and bathrooms are luxurious but blend well with the romantic view of the garden.

The country-style kitchen, moved from the other side of the house to give it a garden view (and now also used as a breakfast room), the boiler room with its bright red and blue pipes, and the cloakroom with its ample, neat space for coats, gumboots and riding boots, including a ledge for stirrups (the owner's wife is a keen huntswoman), are all functional rooms, not tucked away, and as pleasing to see as the rest of the house. Colours are well chosen and even such household problems as where to hang kitchen towels while they are drying have been carefully thought out.

It could be said that the aim of the work at Netherton was to bring it up to date and leave the owners with a country house which would last a lifetime. Apart from the interior decoration, new central heating has been installed, the electricity rewired, additional bathrooms constructed, the roof redone and part of the garden redesigned.

The drawing room

When the architect Raymond Erith drew his plans for the extension of this room (*left*), he took care to keep the existing arched recess so as to avoid having to insert a steel joist. But the arch did pose a problem when the curtains for the room were chosen. Stefanidis' answer was to have high strung curtains falling from the arch, with more curtains hanging from poles to the left and right of the opening where light pours in onto the window seats and squabs. The cotton rug on the floor was woven in Cornwall to match the colour scheme. An ample sofa by the fire, a very large ottoman (both designed by Stefanidis), books in the alcove and a canterbury filled with magazines enhance the comfort of this pleasant golden and cream-coloured room which leads into the garden.

In keeping with the eighteenth-century atmosphere of the house and perhaps with some of the early visitors in mind – it has been said that Nell Gwyn stayed at Netherton and Jane Austen mentions the rectory in a letter – Stefanidis has used his 'Carnation' fabric which is based on an eighteenth-century calico print made for the European market (examples of such prints can be found in the Victoria and Albert Museum archives). The striped curtains were chosen to match this material.

Radiators had already been installed under the window seats and these were retained, with a gap between the seat and the window to allow the heat to rise. Lighting has been carefully arranged at different levels, which Stefanidis considers essential: in this case low for reading, uplighters for general light, and lights above the pictures.

The dining room

The dining room (*p. 36*)– now conveniently near the new kitchen – was once a kitchen and later a drawing room. The present owners wanted it to be red – a happy choice since the room lacked light and life even though the windows gave onto the garden. Today this newly-decorated room, with its crimson two-toned stencilled walls and unlined bright red silk taffeta curtains with knife-pleated pelmets attached (giving all the light possible when open), is dazzling. The Ottoman design came from the Victoria and Albert Museum and was stencilled on the walls by the Czainskis, masters of the craft. Flat stippled or dragged red-painted walls would have lacked the lustre and dimensional effect of this choice. To offset the red of the walls the dado has been painted a rich brown and yet another red. The table-cover is a matching red and the carpet a predominantly brown Aubusson – a foil to all the reds.

A small sitting room

In this elegant but cosy room (*right*) a collection of elephants and watercolours of India and the Far East have set an 'Eastern' style. The strong paisley fabric is Italian but has a Mughal design, and there is a mango-patterned co-ordinating fabric lining the walls. The curtains are strung in the Italian manner – lifting them well up from the window seats. There is a comfortable sofa and a goatskin rug by the fire. The unpretentious furniture here, and throughout most of the house, is Biedermeier.

A man's dressing room

This room (*left*) leads off the master bedroom (*p. 42*). As the owner likes green, his wife chose a bold green Regency striped fabric, and Stefanidis echoed this by painting the walls with large strong stripes which belie the look of wallpaper. The curtains, in a white fabric lined with more green, are very restrained, falling straight under simple box-pleated pelmets. The Biedermeier furniture, a motif in the house, here includes the bed and a chest of drawers; there is also a neoclassical table. For reading there is an adjustable light with a matching green shade.

A guest bedroom

Stefanidis' 'Cosima' chintz, an understated 'brocade', and its co-ordinating fabric, the same design but in muted tones of grey, determined the choice of colours in this room (*right*). The high dado was painted in brown and stone, the cornice in grey, and then an experiment was tried out on the walls: white stripes of varying intensity were painted over a dark brown undercoat. The result is a pleasing grey-brown tint with a faint deceiving stripe that blends with the shades of the 'Cosima' fabrics. The four-poster bed has simple box pleats in 'Cosima', while the co-ordinating fabric is also used for the inside curtains and bedcover, giving a shadowy effect to the interior of the bed. The pull-up blinds, also in 'Cosima', are in the traditional eighteenth-century manner, leaving the garden view uncluttered.

Only light-coloured wood furniture, including a Regency inlaid chest of drawers and a Biedermeier table, was chosen for this room to contrast with the grey and the strong 'Cosima' colours. Rough coconut matting, which has been used throughout the house, covers the floor.

The master bedroom

It is almost a British tradition that the choice of decoration for the master bedroom is a woman's domain, and as a result it is usually very feminine, as here at Netherton. The Stefanidis 'Pelargonium' chintz with its trans-lucent watercolour effect is used for the curtains and also covers the walls. It was designed by the painter Teddy Millington-Drake. The colours — blueish-lilac and white and green on a warm, sunbaked-ochre background — have a Mediter-ranean feel. The gently trailing flowers are white geraniums and the pale violet-blue ones plumbago. The dado is painted the palest powder blue. In contrast, the four-poster bed, dressed in starched white muslin over plain chintz, gives the impression that the hangings have just been casually draped over it. The bedcover is white crochet: no attempt at grandeur here. The furniture is Biedermeier.

Two bathrooms

The bathroom (*left*) that leads off the master bedroom is typical of the Stefanidis approach. The original basin, made in the 1940s, and the taps were kept since he recognizes that much of the design of that period continued the good workmanship of the Edwardian era. A new bath was installed and the marble surround made to match the existing marble round the basin. All other surfaces including the walls were marbelized. Over the basin the mirror has an etched glass panel with a light behind. The curtains reiterate the white of the bedroom but have a narrow grey edging that matches the marble veining. There is a giant towel rail or 'ladder' to make sure that large towels are warm and dry – a Stefanidis trademark. This towel rail has been used again in the bathroom shown on the right, which is crisp brown and white. Towels everywhere in the house are plain white or have just a thin coloured and scalloped edging in cotton. The room has coconut matting on the floor, a pedestal basin installed by Stefanidis and an old-fashioned wooden towel rail for small face towels. Instead of ledges, or a shelf, there is a little bamboo sewing cupboard which was probably made in Japan for the European market.

The eighteenth-century staircase

The hall and the staircase are the most hand-some architectural elements of this former rectory and are said to date back to the eighteenth century. However, the floorboards and beams are part of an earlier seventeenth-century structure. With this in mind, it was indeed bold of Stefanidis to paint the old oak stairs black – shiny black at that. But there is early evidence of the painting of floors and stairs in Britain although it was always more popular in the United States. Today this treatment is back in fashion.

The original choice of colour for the walls was a safe, traditional pale apricot. But after much experimental mixing of Stefanidis' range of colours, a clean sharp blue-grey colour was found in a Sanderson tin which was much more to everyone's liking. The combination of blue with the jet black floorboards and bright white woodwork is striking, and succeeds in evoking an eighteenth-century country house. The simple metal wall lantern is a Stefanidis design.

The print room (*frontispiece*)

The print room, originally the bedroom on the first floor, was the idea of the former owner John Charrington, and the work was executed by the late William MacLaren, a gifted Scottish decorator and painter. It was inspired by the print room at Washington Place in Berkshire, which was destroyed by fire. Stefanidis liked the baroque atmosphere of MacLaren's *trompe-l'oeil* decoration and his new curtains, which are cotton with a moiré pattern, give the impression of being carved out of wood in the rococo tradition. They go well with all the swags, butterflies and bows, and the grey and white cornice. The owner's Louis xv arm-chairs, re-covered in Stefanidis fabric, have now been painted to match the colours of the room, as has the Louis xv Provençal cupboard.

PATMOS

The island of Patmos is a stark, volcanic rock. Rising majestically out of the Aegean Sea, lapped by lazy ripples or buffeted by angry waves, it is crowned with a cluster of whitewashed flat-roofed houses which, like giant steep steps, lead up to the eleventh-century monastery of St John the Divine. Founded by monks from Asia Minor in 1088, the monastery did much to maintain the island's precarious autonomy throughout the Turkish occupation. The monastery's high fortress walls staved off early marauders and later offered security to the rich traders who lived in their shadow in the village of Chora.

Patmos came under Ottoman rule after the fall of Constantinople in 1453. But the Ottoman sultans, in spite of their purges, were tolerant of the Greek Orthodox Patriarch of Constantinople under whose jurisdiction Patmos fell, and they benefited from the island's mercantile prosperity. Much later, in 1912, the island was seized by the Italians and it was not until 1947 – 126 years after the Greek War of Independence – that Patmos returned to Greece. Over the centuries, however, the islanders had clung to their native language and traditions.

Throughout its chequered history Chora has suffered poverty, neglect and destruction, but today its neat whitewashed houses with their brightly painted doors and shutters have replaced the sad scene of derelict roofs and gaping doors. Walking up the cobbled streets the air is scented with a heady mixture of baking herbs emanating from kitchen doors and holy incense and wax from lighted candles that percolate from the myriad of domed Byzantine chapels. Donkeys, carrying everything from fruit to dangerously balanced cupboards and electric cookers, pass through the village whose architecture reads like the pages of a Patmos history book: Cycladic architecture stands side by side with Venetian arches and Byzantine

domes, while the maze of winding stone streets recalls Islamic souks.

The piercing Attic light that casts sharp geometric black shadows on Chora's whitewashed walls, and the restrained island architecture of former fishermen's and sea merchant's houses with their blue, green or ochre doors, windows and shutters and their beamed ceilings, have given Stefanidis an ideal setting, and one perhaps that has unconsciously influenced his work in other countries too. Over ten houses on the island have been restored and decorated by him, one newly built. And having taken great care to train the local carpenter and the midwife-mattress-maker now the upholsterer – Stefanidis has set a style and left an imprint for others to follow. At least forty houses have now been restored in Patmos for foreigners and mainland Greeks but what marks Stefanidis' houses is

that he has consistently avoided folklore and instead followed the austere simplicity of the vernacular architecture. All his houses have strictly maintained the traditional Greek island style: island furniture has been copied and adapted, island hangings carefully stitched and spread on beds and sofas, island lace used for edging and lace covers dipped in tea as Greek grandmothers used to do.

Perhaps most effective of all is the way in which Stefanidis has used the piercing shafts of light that cut through his windows, trellis screens and doors. His use of trelliswork for cupboards, tables, doors and shutters is the very essence of his island style. In the hot summer the trelliswork allows the air to flow; and when used for doors or screens it filters the light, throwing up dappled patterns on the whitewashed walls. The lattice-work on the cabinet (*left*) must have originated in the 'mousharabia' of the Islamic world where windows overlooking the street had trellised screens so that the ladies of the harem might look out but avoid men's stares. Stefanidis sketched the cabinet for the carpenter with whom he had worked for many years and who never needed detailed working drawings, but he forgot to mention that the doors must open. When completed it turned out to be purely decorative.

Like the merchants who returned from their travels bringing goods from countries they had visited, so Stefanidis has brought furniture, rugs and decorative items from other lands. Yet there is nothing ostentatious about his houses: he has always been bound by the simplicity that the thick white walls and scrubbed floors demand. Having in mind the island's future he has respected its past and has given the new owners, who seek in Patmos a refuge from the hustle of contemporary life, both modern comforts and a repose in keeping with Patmos's monastic purity, for this is the island of the Revelation of St John the Divine.

The library

The view of the library (*p. 48*) shows how Stefanidis mixes imported furniture with local furniture and furnishings. The nineteenth-century Mughal cabinet with multiple drawers was japanned in England where the stand was fitted. The eighteenth-century Italian mirror above was found on the island, as were the small vases and the Turkish repoussé silver bowl. Although some floors in Greek island houses are painted, here the unpolished floorboards have been scrubbed with soap and water in the more traditional manner. The two wooden door stoppers were once the legs of an Arabian bed. The library chair unfolds to become a ladder.

The courtyard

The covered courtyard (*left*) with its wooden beamed ceiling has steps leading to the first floor and out onto a series of descending terraces. In the foreground is a stone wellhead below which, stretching the full length of the courtyard, lies a huge cistern for storing water. Just behind it are two large jars once used for storing oil and olives. The floor is covered with traditional terracotta tiles made on the island. The craft had died out when John Stefanidis began to work on Patmos but has now been resuscitated. The wavy pattern is made by pressing four fingers on the tile before the clay is set. The white line at the base of the walls can be seen in many Greek island houses: it is the result of 'tidying-up' the drips from the annual whitewashing in a neat line. This creates a flowing effect, much less rigid than skirting, and makes the wall appear to continue until it meets the tiles. The lantern clasped ceremoniously in an outstretched hand is Venetian. There are other lanterns which are borne out to the terraced garden in the evening. Until recently, before the advent of electricity, people carried lanterns in the streets at night. A wooden rail by the door is for shawls which are needed on cool evenings; another is for hats – protection against the Mediterranean sun.

The parlour

Leading off the courtyard is the parlour (*p. 51*) lit by a gap in the ceiling through which light pours down from the terrace above. This local architectural feature has been used by Stefanidis in other houses on the island (*see p. 113*). Cushions covered with Rhodian and Turkish embroideries are scattered on the old Patmos sofa and a blue kelim from Thrace in northern Greece lies on the floor. A pair of seventeenth-century maps, one of Rome, the other of Venice, hang on the wall above two locally-carved chests. The two eighteenth-century Italian provincial chairs with rush seats suit this room, as do the small Regency table and the old Flora Danica plates displayed in the glass-fronted cupboard.

The upstairs sitting rooms

The detail of the sitting room (*left*) demonstrates again how well furniture and objects from different cultures blend with the rigid simplicity of Patmos's indigenous pieces. The Arabian chest from the Hadramout has a close affinity to the carved wooden island doors, and the modern decorative work by the Greek sculptor Takis on the chest complements the gold-encrusted Indian icon.

The second sitting room (*above*) has Stefa-nidis' trellis tables and rush-seated stools. These stools, made for him on the island and on Rhodes, are easy to move and surprisingly comfortable; they were once found all over Greece and the Levant. One of the Empire sofas in this room is an original from Patmos, the others are copies. They are plainly upholstered in an unbleached cotton with cushions made like mattresses. The wooden shutters, which on Patmos are always on the inside, have been left unpainted. This is because they looked so good when stripped and scrubbed, and they have now acquired a golden patina. A seventeenth-century ivory and ebony chest with two candlesticks stands against the white walls.

A guest bedroom

Stefanidis' Patmos bedrooms have an almost monastic simplicity: their lightness and the traditional blue and white colours he uses are cool and refreshing.

This small bedroom has space for a large bedside table which is covered in a cream striped Turkish silk with gold embroidery. Above it is a practical Anglepoise reading light with a metal shade (paper shades disintegrate during the damp winter months). The bedhangings are plain white cotton bought by the yard and trimmed in crochet, and the cover is again crochet. The steel bed is nineteenth-century Italian. Such beds, often seen on the islands, must at one time have been as plentiful as Thonet chairs and were found all over Greece and the Middle East.

A tiny bathroom

Despite its size, this tiny bathroom includes a lavatory, bidet, basin, shower (from which this picture was taken) and a stone bench to sit on. The room is lit by diamond sunlight shafts that filter through the white trellis door in the daytime and by the two functional brass bulkhead lights at night. The stone floor is outlined in whitewash as on island pavements. The green mirror is one of the many adaptations of local designs which Stefanidis and his gifted carpenter have fashioned. The curtains, hung over poles, are plain Indian cotton saris.

A guest bedroom

The blue and white guest bedroom has a Stefanidis-designed four-poster bed; the shell design of the locally-worked crochet bedspread allows the blue undercover to show through. The delicate muslin curtains have looped tapes in the seventeenth-century manner and can be raised or lowered. The dressing table is covered in cream silk with an elaborate Turkish fringe; its provincial Empire mirror is supported by two dolphins. The Stefanidis chairs, called 'Malcontenta', were inspired by those in the Palladian villa of that name near Venice (*see also pp. 58–9*) and, it is believed, were designed by Alberti. In a second courtyard past the blue painted door a tame duck often waddles in to check on guests at breakfast time.

A garden sitting room

Although the garden sitting room looks as if it has been there for years – it is so solid and cool – it was originally a chicken coop and has been entirely rebuilt. New terracotta tiles were laid on the floor and small windows in the vernacular style were cut out so as to throw shafts of sunlight on the whitewashed walls. A new island door – a door within a door – leads to the garden.

The table on the right, which has a Stefanidis lamp with a metal shade on it, is made of cement and has a wooden top. It was inspired by the stone tables in monastery refectories, as can be found on Mount Athos and on Patmos itself in the monastery of St John the Divine. Here again is the 'Malcontenta' chair (*see also p. 57*) standing by a blue and white Indian durrie: Stefanidis prefers the dry coolness of cotton for these carpets, which are now mostly made of wool. (Durries were originally made by prisoners in India: they were given designs to copy in jail – either time-honoured Indian or English patterns.) Stefanidis' two 'Beistigui' chairs, based on the Mexican collector Charles de Beistigui's library chairs of the 50s, are loose covered in white cotton, with cushions in Stefanidis' 'Esrajim Stripe'. The seat is a naive interpretation of a Louis XVI sofa, and the pale lilac cushions are cut out of an Indian lungi. The screen covered with prints of figures in Greek and Turkish costumes was found in Athens.

59

The dining room and terraces

When the day's salt water and sun have been showered away, dinner is served either in the downstairs room, outside in a walled courtyard or in the garden. For formal occasions the whitewashed dining room (*pp. 60–1*) is used; silver candlesticks stand on a trestle table covered by a linen cloth with sharp folds reminiscent of medieval paintings.

For a more informal dinner a table is set in the vine- and plumbago-covered pergola (*above*). A traditional island sofa can be seen in the background, Stefanidis' rush-seated Patmos stools are used instead of chairs and the table-cloth is a Stefanidis print. Flickering light comes from Turkish concertina lanterns which although very decorative catch fire easily.

Outside on the garden terrace (*right*) there is a carpet to sit on – cross-legged if you wish – as if you were in some Asian country. This corner of the garden is devoted to sitting – for lunch, if it is not too hot, and in the cool evenings for chatting wrapped up in shawls. The bright blue and white mattress cushions pick up the tumbling blue plumbago, and the black Libyan rug looks well with the green leaves and whitewashed bark of the lemon trees (the local protection against insects) and the profusion of lavender and roses.

THE BANK OF ENGLAND

The history of the Bank can be traced back to 1694 when, following a suggestion from a Scottish merchant William Paterson, an Act of Parliament approved the setting up of a company to lend capital to the government (the official title was 'The Governor and Company of the Bank of England'). The government of the day, hard pressed to finance the war against France, needed to borrow money which the new Bank was able to supply. However, by 1797 government demands for gold from the bank were so heavy that the new institution was forced into a 'Restriction Period' (which lasted until 1821) and it no longer paid out gold for notes. This move was depicted in a cartoon by the witty political caricaturist James Gillray who was to give the Bank the affectionate name it carries to this day. Gillray's cartoon shows the young Prime Minister William Pitt – his arms outstretched – leaping to embrace a horrified old lady dressed in pound notes, and his caption read: 'Political Ravishment or the Old Lady of Threadneedle Street in danger'.

The Threadneedle Street site, which was the first permanent site owned by the Bank – previously it had operated from rented premises – was purchased for the sum of £15,000, and it included the home of Sir John Houblon, the first Governor, and the adjoining premises. By 1734 the building of the Bank was completed from plans by a little-known architect, George Samson, but throughout the years the structure has undergone many alterations. Sir Robert Taylor was the second architect to work on the bank and he extended the building. He was followed by Sir John Soane who made further extensive additions to what he referred to as a building in 'a grand style of Palladian simplicity'. The last major rebuilding programme was carried out between 1925 and 1939 by Sir Herbert Baker who gave the Bank its present imposing structure while still retaining the Palladian theme.

When, in 1985, the Governor of the Bank Robin Leigh-Pemberton decided to give 'The Old Lady' a face-lift – the rooms on the first floor, known as the Governor's parlours, were due for decoration – he approached John Stefanidis and asked him to put forward some suggestions. Perhaps it was felt that he would show due reverence to the Bank's classical architecture and at the same time understand the modern use of the rooms. Stefanidis made two presentations for this project to the Governor and the élite phalanx of officials who were to make the final decision. One presentation was so formal that, in Stefanidis' words, 'it would have required the Bank's liveried attendants with their bright pink gold buttoned tail coats, red waistcoats and black trousers to stand permanently in line'; the other, which was chosen, was more in keeping with the functions of the building today, while at the same time returning it to its former grandeur.

A Palladian window

The 'undressed' window (*left*) belongs to the committee room (*p. 66*). It is an excellent example of how Baker carried out the brief he received from the Bank in 1925 which was to follow, incorporate and reproduce Sir John Soane's style. Over the columns a visual trick is achieved by using double urns as 'shadows' or 'reflections'. The urns inside are of alabaster, while those outside are of stone; the stone ones are of course visible through the window panes. Steel has been used in the structure of the window but its design – a 1920s version of a beautiful Palladian window – has been preserved.

The landing

Classical grandeur meets guests now as they take the staircase built by Baker which opens onto the severe stone wall landing (*opposite*). Here Stefanidis wanted a dignified approach and rearranged the busts of George III (1812), Robert Peel (1852), William III (1811) and William Cotton, a Governor of the Bank (1855). He also removed all unnecessary furniture and gave the window a sculptured effect by hanging rich beige silk damask curtains in accurate period style.

The dining room

The Governor normally uses two round tables when entertaining in this room (*overleaf above*) and these are formally set with white starched tablecloths and highly polished silver. Although Stefanidis has said that by far the smartest aspect here is the white-gloved liveried stewards, his work has brought both light and a sense of restrained grandeur to the dining room. The walls and ceilings have been painted in shades of white picked out in gold;

he has re-covered the chairs in small patterned horsehair; and he has designed two very practical sideboards in the Soane manner which not only keep dishes warm but look as if they have always been in the room.

The committee room

The colours for the committee room (*left below*) were chosen because of the predominantly blue carpet which was made for the room in 1928. The wall and ceiling were painted in shades of blue and white picked out in gold, and a darker shade of blue was used to accentuate the dado. Stefanidis rehung the pictures in all the rooms: the one over the mantelpiece is Augustus John's portrait of Montagu Norman, the Governor who held office for the longest period of time (from 1920 to 1944). It hangs simply but rather dramatically from a gold spear. Over the bookcases – which are in fact cupboards – Stefanidis added *girandoles* which were designed specially for the room, and are based on photographs dating from 1930 in the Bank's archives. Round the room the decorative plaques are picked out in gold and white: one encases a clock, others represent Mercury, Moneta (Juno), Honos, Securitas Publica and Minerva. The glittering late eighteenth-century chandelier is rumoured to have come from a Rothschild house, while the additional functional lamps were found in the Bank's basement store. The original blue baize tablecover was kept as it makes an excellent working surface. The chairs were re-covered in pale blue imitation suede, one of the few synthetic fabrics that Stefanidis finds works well.

The anteroom

This grand room (*right*) is used by Directors who assemble there before Court meetings, and

also for entertaining on formal occasions. Crimson red silk damask covers the walls and is used again for the sumptuous curtains and festoon blinds – a treatment in keeping with the *en suite* decoration of the seventeenth and eighteenth centuries when walls, curtains and furniture were covered in the same fabric to achieve unity and an opulent effect.

When Stefanidis began to work on this room, it lacked symmetry owing to the frequent alterations that had taken place. There was only one window with a dim outlook and a fireplace off-centre. His initial plan was to try to restore Baker's original structure, with vaulted ceilings – even including the lunettes painted for the room which depicted the building work in progress at the Bank. But, alas, the pictures were by then scattered all over the building, and since Baker's time the room had changed irreparably. Moreover, air conditioning had been installed in the ceiling and the reconstruction work could have created some security problems.

In the end Stefanidis had to alter his plans. The ceiling and cornice were rebuilt and gilded which allowed the air conditioning to be hidden and for four chandeliers to be hung. These, along with the new ceiling and the careful positioning of furniture and pictures, have given balance to the room. The corner of the anteroom in the picture shows one of the earliest oval desks of the Chippendale period (1770), a gilt Chippendale mirror and eighteenth-century chairs. The small bookcase and clock of the '*Retour d'Egypte*' period, along with other items of furniture in the room, were found in the Bank's basement store by Stefanidis. The portrait is of Sir Robert Clayton by Lorenzo da Castro. He was a director of the Bank of England from 1702 to 1707 and had formerly been Lord Mayor. The Regency candelabra were given a Brighton Pavilion air with a leaf motif in their glass tops.

TORONTO TOWN HOUSE

When Stefanidis undertook the decoration of this house in Toronto he already knew his clients' taste well as he had completed work on their country house in England. In a town that boasts some seven miles of covered passages and shopping centres against the rigours of the winter, Stefanidis had also to bear in mind, when drawing up his plans and choosing furniture and fabrics, the extreme climatic changes in Canada – the snow-bound winters and hot summers. The house had to look outwards in summer and inwards in winter.

Now that the project is finished, it is interesting to see how Stefanidis and his team brought together furniture and decorative objects from London, New York, Milan and Paris, and how this period house has been transformed so that it no longer has the atmosphere of a tree-lined suburb. Flowing floral stencils with an Eastern flavour, plain gathered cotton fabrics on the walls, specially designed bold Stefanidis fabrics on chairs and for bed hangings, curtains and blinds, and the distinguished pieces of furniture (often in pairs) around the house, all contribute to making this family house both elegant and practical. There is luxury it is true, but it is not ostentatious; there is also comfort and warmth, but above all there is order and continuity in design – essential rules which Stefanidis respects, which make the Edwardian-style house a contrast to Toronto's skyscrapers.

The hall

A stone effect for the walls similar to that at Fort Belvedere (p. 16) was chosen for the hall. The blue and white plant bowls and the plate pick up the colour in the blue and gold mirror surround (*opposite*), with its crystal candle sconce. This is one of a pair of oval Irish mirrors that hang over two plain eighteenth-century marble-topped side tables. The pillared portico is flanked by two busts on plinths and a pair of stools are placed next to them. The floor, composed of rectangular stone slabs laid diagonally to give depth, is plain and easy to maintain. The total concept is classical, simple and unaffected.

The drawing room

The strong, predominantly red pattern of Stefanidis' 'Bokhara' fabric (*far right*), based on a Suzani embroidery which covers the table (*p. 74*), is used in this room (*pp. 70–1*) with intent. Another interpretation of the design has been stencilled on to the walls, giving shape and height, and creating a rich, enclosed atmosphere reminiscent of the floral tents used by the Ottomans during the siege of Vienna in 1529. The design appears again – in this case specially adapted as a medallion pattern – on the Louis xv chairs (*right*). These were originally covered in regal green velvet which Stefanidis found 'too pompous' so he changed them. The reverse of the chair backs is covered in eighteenth-century fashion in a plainer material – in this case Stefanidis' 'Esrajim Stripe'.

Symmetry is added to this room by the careful placing of a pair of antique tables on either side of the green silk striped sofa, a pair of mirrors and a pair of commodes. The decorative gilt mirrors are eighteenth-century as are the commodes of a restrained design in the English manner. Two Empire incense burners stand on the commode and two important drawings, one by Giacometti and the other by Van Gogh, are very simply displayed – on purpose – just as if they had been temporarily propped up there. The drawings and paintings in this room have all been chosen for their 'light' quality. A blue Chinese jar stands on a Stefanidis plinth which has a painted porphry pattern in clear blue – an antidote to the reds in the room.

Though not shown in the pictures, the room has a marbelized fireplace and red-covered Beistigui chairs (*see also p. 58–9*). There is, too, a small upright sofa, useful for extra seating, and a large ottoman – both covered in red. A Faoul Dufy painting hangs over the fireplace with a large gouache by Toulouse Lautrec on the side wall. Within the curve of the bay window there is a huge sofa covered in 'Bokhara'.

A view to the hall

Looking from the drawing room towards the hall (*left*), the 'Bokhara' walls and the Suzani embroidery tablecover contrast with the austerity of the hall's 'stone' walls and floor. A silver polo trophy serves as a large flower vase: it stands on an eighteenth-century English marble-topped gilt console table above which hangs a Balthus drawing. The handsome chair is English.

In the drawing room, a simple lamp lights the mixture of objects – some valuable, some not – on the table: an early Picasso drawing of mother and child, a group of Chinese bowls and a specimen vase of flowers.

The dining room

When Stefanidis first saw the dining room (*right*) he decided to keep the existing panelled walls and two cupboards which already contained some of Mason's Ironstone plates. More pieces were added and the collection was lit. The panelling was painted in tones of buff and a new overmantel with a mirror and a broken pediment was added to the fireplace. The *garniture de cheminée* was found in Paris, and the Georgian silver candlesticks were bought at a New York auction. Warmth and colour were added by the purchase in New York of the splendid carpet; while the sober traditional extending table came from London. The chairs are a Stefanidis design – always fashioned to fit the size of the table. Although this room brings together antiques which were specially purchased, they look as if they have always been there and this simple, restrained room has become lively and welcoming.

A guest bedroom

'Emma', a very English chintz inspired by an eighteenth-century Spitalfields silk fragment in the Victoria and Albert Museum, sets the fresh tone of this room. The four-poster bed is hung with it in the traditional English manner and lined with Stefanidis' 'Angela', a co-ordinating fabric. In the American fashion the pillows are piled up and instead of a bedcover there is a pale cotton blanket cover with a white and blue butterfly design. At the foot of the bed stands a *chaise-longue* also covered in 'Angela'. The dressing table and the smaller functional table are decorated in the eighteenth-century fashion with organza flounces – like summer dresses, and on the pale blue-green walls, a series of pretty plates has been hung. Four Italian provincial Empire chairs in parcel-gilt, bought in Milan and covered in ice-blue woven cotton, contrast with the frills of the room.

The main bedroom

The walls of this bedroom (*left*) are covered with yards and yards of the miniature designs of 'Vermiculé' fabric which is gathered and fixed with rods at top and bottom. This material derives from the background design to an old French print of the Tree of Life and has been used for the bathroom walls and curtains. The amusing pink chairs were copies made by Stefanidis of an original French *crapaud*-style chair of 1840. The sofa and ottoman were designed to match. Some of the owners' collection of china is set out on the mantelpiece – an Irish country-house touch. The half-tester bed, with a Regency *chaise-longue* at its foot in the traditional manner, was chosen instead of a four-poster as being more suited for a low-ceilinged American room. A bed as wide as this would have needed posts out of all proportion to the room. The bed hangings are gathered with frills and pleats as are the curtains. All the frills are pinked and scalloped; the linings of the frills on the bed are made of coral silk, while the linings of the curtain frills are chintz.

The library

This corner of the library (*right*) is a place for reading in comfort and for watching television. On the floor is a rare kelim which, unusually, contains different types of weaving.

The bay window has a large comfortable sofa, and traditional armchairs with pull-up footstools. All their silk cushions bear out Stefanidis' strict rule of 'avoiding pointed ears'. Adjustable lamps give good light for reading, while the lacquer bookcase on wheels is a familiar piece in many of his houses. Here it stands below the window and serves as an 'anchor'. The shutters – reminiscent of seventeenth-century Dutch interiors – are used to cover the windows instead of curtains. The large-scale wire-fronted bookcase was inspired by a Regency design.

GLENBOGLE

A log house, surrounded here by fluttering daffodils, is an unusual sight. Although more often built in the United States and Scandinavia, it fits surprisingly well into the Scottish landscape. Some years ago a grand house on the site burnt down and the owners, after much soul-searching, decided against rebuilding their stately home. Instead they purchased a house from Scandinavia in the form of a kit of numbered logs which were carefully assembled on the spot. Today for the present owners, who inherited the house from their parents, the setting is ideal. They are very keen fishermen and what could be better than to overlook the River Dee – that prestigious fisherman's paradise?

Originally the house was divided into two with the family living in one side and the gillie and his wife living in the other. When Stefanidis began work he knocked it into one as the gillie had been given a house nearby.

The tackle room

This room, where boots and fishing tackle are kept, is well lit by utilitarian lights. It is mainly a man's room and a bar; boxes for flies, shelves specially constructed for rods, sensible, solid, upright chairs and a cork floor make it well organized and highly functional.

The sitting room

This room (*above*), which exudes a fragrant scent from the log walls, both here and throughout the house, has to accommodate quite a number of people. There are always guests staying and friends dropping in. With this in mind, Stefanidis lined the walls with sofas and designed comfortable window seats, using plain colours and small patterns for the upholstery. A collection of Graham Sutherland prints is grouped above one of the sofas. Wall lights are fixed on either side of the fireplace – something that Stefanidis would not usually do – but here they take up less room and make the

fireside the best place to read. In front of the fire a rug remains even though it is 'a little boring', but Stefanidis believes that no room should be 'perfect'. Variations are essential for a more natural atmosphere.

The dining room

Black-faced sheep, in etchings by Henry Moore, and Highland cattle by Edward Burra, look down on the table (*right*) from the wood-clad walls. The loose-covered Stefanidis chairs and the tablecloth in his 'Fish' fabric are an appropriate accompaniment to any Highland meal.

The central hall

The central hall fans out into the dining room, sitting room, kitchen and tackle room. A plain wooden staircase with cut-out banisters, in keeping with the wood-clad walls, leads to the floor above. Stefanidis has used similar, almost child-like cut-out banisters again on Patmos and on other projects. Based on an Indian temple screen motif, they are an example of the repetition of primary design across all frontiers. Proof, too, of how good design can be used in almost any surroundings. Here the ancient naive inspiration fits with ease into a modern fishing lodge because of its purity; and blends so well with the surroundings that it passes almost unnoticed.

Although a great deal of the existing oak furniture was in bad repair, Stefanidis decided that it suited the lodge and chose a small gate-legged table in the hall, and in the dining room he made use of the old dining table as a side table. The chairs, like those in the dining room, are a Stefanidis design and have loose covers with bows in his 'Fish' fabric. Coconut matting is spread on the floor and continued through-out the house. Right up the stairs the walls are hung with painted prize fish, trophies of earlier family fishermen, leaving you in no doubt about the lodge's main function. Indeed, as you enter the hall the atmosphere and the objects make this abundantly clear.

The bedroom

An austere, painted four-poster bed by Stefanidis has hangings in his own country check fabric tied with bows to the framework of the bed. The same material is used for the reefed-up blinds and the dressing table and coordinates well with his 'Poppy' fabric which covers the stool. In small rooms, he finds that it is often an advantage to repeat the same pattern on furniture and windows in the *en suite* manner favoured by eighteenth-century decorators. The collection of china and the Chinese chairs were bought for the room by the owners.

LOOKING
AT
ROOMS

HALLS

Early eighteenth-century records of English town houses describe halls as places where servants lingered, and in keeping with this function their decoration usually consisted of urns, statues and sometimes sporting pictures, but rarely family portraits or important paintings. In grand country houses it was different: the hall often served as a dining room and was a place where 'breakfast battledore and shuttlecock and the harpsichord, *go on at the same time without* molesting one another', to quote Mrs Delany's vivid description in 1733 (*see also p. 17*).

Halls have always had an air of expectancy – of anticipation before the curtain rises to give the first glimpse of the owner and the costume of his house. Classic grandeur, marble floors, swirling rococo staircases, a roaring open hearth or the restricted feeling of a Lutyens 'lead in' lobby to a hall and staircase, all have

their interpretation today even though the dining room has moved elsewhere, hall space is smaller and no servants wait at the door. Stefanidis' 1980s treatment of halls borrows from the past as he brings them into the present.

An Italianate hall

Surprisingly, this Italianate hall in Eaton Square with its pink and dapple grey Post-Modernist columns and golden light reflected from ceiling strips of mirrored glass looks as if it has always been there: in actual fact it is completely new. After Stefanidis had gutted the flat, he designed a lobby leading on the one side to the elevator and on the other to the front door. The floor is marble in a chequered pattern of pale grey and beige – black and white was avoided as being, Stefanidis said,

'too jumpy' for such a small space. The console table with a marbelized top extends from the wall, and was carved out of wood but painted to look like stone. It has a double function as it hides the radiators and is a place to stand things on – flowers, books and letters.

The decision on the colour for the walls came after the painters were asked for boards showing various shades, and a bold scheme of marbelized Venetian pink, reminiscent of the 'Marmorino' technique, was chosen. In Stefanidis' opinion, 'Italians use colour with bravado but English painters, more used to the traditional restraint of English architecture, are more timid.' The classical motif of panelled 'secret' doors (there are three of these which lead into the rest of the apartment) carry the eye forward towards the light of the drawing room doors, a 'lead in' which has been repeated on a smaller scale in the riverside flat (*p. 33*).

A Regency hall

Typical of London's small Regency houses, this house has a small, narrow, dark hall and a traditional plain staircase (*left*). But as it had a garden, Stefanidis immediately created light by opening up the vista to the garden through a large window which reaches down to the floor. It is a sash window in keeping with the others in the house. Now as you enter the front door your eye is carried forward – through the narrow hall to the space and light of the garden. The colour of the walls is a radiant yellow with a sponged effect – this again reflects light. The lantern is one of the mosque lanterns which Stefanidis often adapts and his aim here was to have something that was not pompous. The carved 1930s chair is covered in an unusual *petit-point* embroidery depicting blue and white china pots.

An island lobby

This hall (*right*) is also a lobby between two rooms – a link between two areas of light. It acts as a hall on one side where a door leads through a short passage to the street; it also serves as a lobby to a large sitting room through two half-glazed doors (only one is shown). The floor is covered with tatami matting, often used in Europe in the eighteenth century; there is a Stefanidis trellis cupboard for stereo and drinks and a well-placed folding Mandarin chair. The walls have been dramatically painted in greys, blue and yellow by Teddy Millington-Drake. The sun and moon, pyramidal shapes and other forms of symbolism add wonder to this small dark space which was once a bedroom with the traditional Patmos half-glazed doors (*see p. 115*).

Painted walls in an Athens suburb

The hall on the left is in a 1930s house in an Athens suburb, and it is the antithesis of Stefanidis' eighteenth-century hall on the right. The former was built in the Athenian version of the European architecture of the 1930s and Stefanidis wanted to emphasize this spirit when he remodelled it. Removing a wrought-iron staircase he replaced it with one made of mortar and plaster to give a bold continuous sweep. A stereo and bar area with a fireplace was arranged behind mirrored sliding doors to be shut out when not in use.

The whole space has been treated in a modern, light way and the large mural by Teddy Millington-Drake in pale colours follows the theme. There is no attempt at secretive lighting; instead, the downlighters are prominent as they shed their sharp beams on the painted walls and leave the stairs awash with light. This hall is a typical example of how Stefanidis treats a large space with simplicity.

A contemporary approach to the eighteenth century

This is the hall in Stefanidis' London house in Cheyne Walk (*right*). Black and white marble slabs cover the large floor area – something the designer himself might have carried out but in fact he found it had already been laid by Sir Hugh Lane, a former owner, in about 1910. The pillars which were painted white have now been marbelized a warm ochre colour and in search for more light – as always in Stefanidis' work – the staircase walls, once dead grey, have now been painted a carefully

textured ochre. A dark emerald green runner is laid up the stripped pine stairs and the dado has been painted charcoal grey. The walls in the hall are also textured but in a silver-grey colour to complement the *papier peint* panels which are hung like grisaille. In both cases the paint is 'dry' like water paint and has a transparent luminous quality. The low dado, which only runs at one end of the hall, is kept light by the grey *faux bois*. The bust – which could have always stood there – is English of the seven-

teenth century; the nineteenth-century laurel-wreath mirror has been painted grey. A chair in cut velvet stands beside the spacious coat cupboard which has a wire and fabric door to allow the air to flow through. The shadow on the ochre walls comes from a Stefanidis lantern on the first floor. This lantern, which has been used in several of his houses, is like the stark skeleton of an ancient lantern: it has no glass, just four candlesticks with clip-on brass shades and real candles – to be lit on festive occasions.

the designer David Hicks. The picture on the left shows the view into the hall through its two polyurethane columns. These, Stefanidis explains, are 'fun, as they fit one on top of the other in a multicoloured way, and like children's cubes you can rearrange them when and how you wish'. The dramatic giant picture, which covers the whole wall from floor to ceiling, is by the Post-Realist painter Malcolm Morley and has as its theme Vermeer's *The Artist in his Studio*.

The stone stairs were stripped bare and the walls were given a rough surface by the painters who, under Stefanidis' instructions, used brooms and the whole length of their arms to form the circular strokes. A focal point against this freestyle wall is the bold painting by the Pop artist Tom Wesselmann. At night it is lit by an aluminium picture light.

Creating an illusion with paint

Both these contrasting halls (*overleaf*) were treated in a similar way, the principle being the use of very shiny paint which reflects and confuses the eye, giving an illusion of depth in the London hall and breadth in the Paris corridor.

The picture on page 97 is of the entrance to a London basement flat leading towards a courtyard. The hall space has been dealt with very simply. Light enters through the glass apartment door, and an unobtrusive console – which Stefanidis says is 'now somewhat dated but like most things may well come back in fashion' – has been painted white; the cut-out panel on the wall masks the radiator and the electricity metre. The brilliant shiny paint throughout dispels the basement atmosphere.

Similar distraction through the use of paint is shown in the corridor of a Paris flat on page 96. But here, because the space is long and very narrow, the walls have been faceted and the ceiling constructed at different heights. The walls, which are painted in different colours – pink and orange – lead to a lobby where a tall, upright painting catches the eye.

Moveable columns in Chester Square

There were no good architectural features in this Edwardian house except for a stone staircase and even that was weak. Once the residence of a fashionable doctor who rode about town in a Rolls Royce, it was a sad relic of the past. Filled with Edwardian paraphernalia of poor quality, it provided no comfort, no heating and just one bathroom. John Stefanidis retained only the decorative ceiling from a former billiard room for the new kitchen (*p. 150*) and then started anew. In the hall he pulled down a partition so that the front door opened straight out into the large hall and he 'limed' the floor white in an eighteenth-century manner – a tip he had been given by

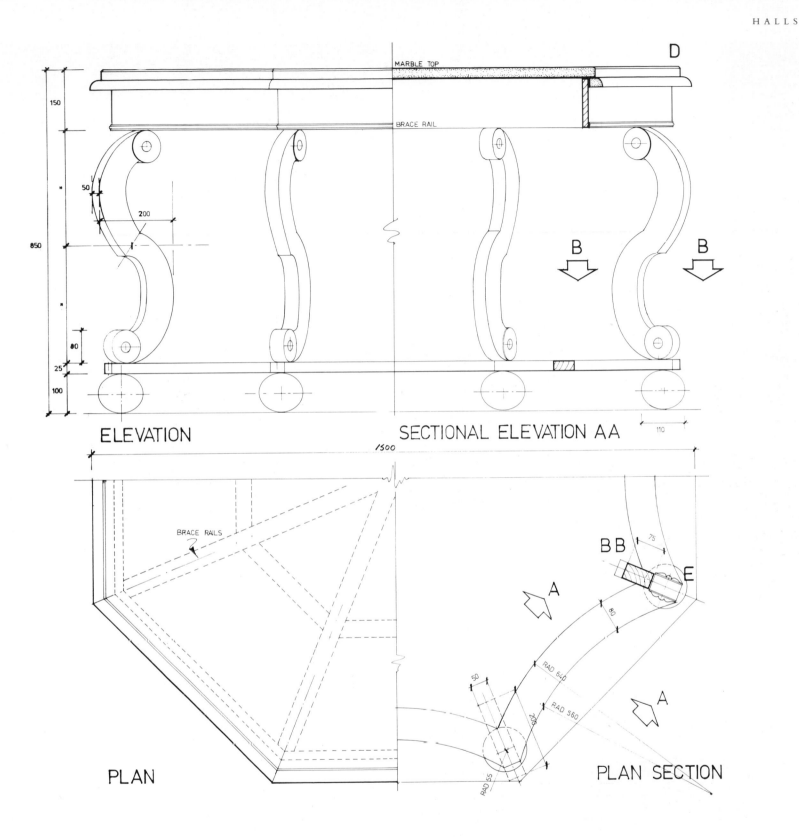

ELEVATION SECTIONAL ELEVATION AA

PLAN PLAN SECTION

The hall as sitting room

When he began work on this Norman Shaw Surrey mansion, Stefanidis decided that the large hall, reminiscent of the days when halls were used as living rooms and dining rooms, was 'too important to ignore'. He realized that he had to combine his client's taste with respect for the architecture of the building. Antique furniture was chosen – some Regency and some of a later date. The view looking down the staircase shows the glazed-in sitting area which has generous seating space, a fireplace and a bar. The windows were all redesigned to open out into the garden. As one comes down the stairs the visual target of the hall is the Stefanidis table. It has been used elsewhere in different wood (*see p. 16*), but here it is painted off-white and beige and has a stone top. A meticulous working drawing of the table is shown above.

Greek simplicity

Tradition has been revered in this Patmos hall
(*left*) which has whitewashed walls, an old tiled
floor and just one simple white-cushioned
wooden sofa. A splash of colour from the
Bokhara embroidery on the wall provides a
focal point as one steps through the lobby door.
Above this there is a shelf with carefully positioned pottery from the island of Samos –
proving Stefanidis' maxim that 'how you place
objects is as important as how you arrange
furniture'.

International style in New York

This hall of a New York penthouse (*right*),
surrounded with terraces and aglow with light,
shows a dramatic contrast in style to the hall
opposite. The remodelled flat has tranquillity
and a sense of space – the right background for
the owner's collection of contemporary art
such as the Frank Stella painting. The floor is
grander than that of Chester Square (*pp. 94–5*)
yet treated in a similar 'limed' fashion, and has
been given a pale wash. The lounger-sofa in the
sitting room beyond is a Stefanidis design of
the early 1970s.

DRAWING ROOMS

Exactly when a drawing room became a drawing room is difficult to say but in the early 1600s it was a hall or parlour, later that century it was included in the enfilade of rooms in the state apartments and then gradually in England it became a room to 'withdraw in' – more private and more comfortable. By the early eighteenth century the drawing room, usually with a feminine air, began to be a room for ladies to gather, for the family and for friends; it was no longer designed mainly for grand and formal entertaining as in France and America. Today the drawing room, often known as the sitting room, combines the functions of the elegant and often gilded saloon on the *piano nobile*, with those of the library and the music room.

In the past fashion, mostly inspired by France, ruled the design and decoration of the drawing room. Fashion dictated its space or clutter and its function. When fashions changed the rooms changed too. In Stefanidis' contemporary rendering of drawing rooms it is often impossible to discern fashionable influences since they are all so varied. Instead, they show a balance between what the architecture of the room demands and what use is to be made of the space; to this Stefanidis has added his expertise and his use of colour and light. The photographs which follow illustrate certain aspects of his drawing rooms, but cannot show the way he works which is mobile and selective as he builds up a whole room: adding sofas or chairs for comfort or leaving empty space to rest the eye; giving more light for reading and grander or less grand furniture, hangings and decoration, with the use of the room always in mind. But the photographs do give an interesting picture of the multitude of cheerful, refined, cool and elegant designs he has given his drawing rooms, always taking into account the country or town they are in, the climate, the light and their use.

The saloon at Auborn Chase

An imposing columned portico and a sweeping staircase with delicate pale lemon and white stucco walls lead one along a passage to the saloon (*overleaf*) on the first floor of this Palladian house. A tall mahogany door opens into this room flooded with light – the colours of 'a ripe pomegranate that has burst', in Stefanidis' words. This effect is achieved not only by the spectrum of colours and fabrics, but on closer analysis it is the general harmony and balance that the designer creates so successfully.

This room was probably once a gaming room, or perhaps used to promenade in, as were the long galleries in earlier houses such as Montacute in Somerset. In the nineteenth century the saloon was divided up into three or four bedrooms and it was only some twenty years ago that it was reconstructed. The original coved ceiling measuring 25 by 9 metres was uncovered, and two fireplaces were installed on either side of the door, giving better balance to a room with five windows along one wall and none facing it.

Stefanidis' plan for this grand room included using some of the existing furniture and decorative items and adding others of his own design so as to establish the correct symmetrical balance which is always in his 'eye'. The existing carpet, made for the room about twenty years earlier, was in his opinion 'too large to change' so he worked round it. The unsightly radiators which had been installed below the windows were removed and set below the floors with brass grilles. Though it does not look that way, the polished oak floorboards are new and the oak surround now enhances the carpet – avoiding that 'fitted' Edwardian look. The sadly sagging sofas and armchairs were immensely comfortable and therefore just re-upholstered and re-covered. Pairs, double pairs, triple pairs of furniture and sitting islands were on Stefanidis' mental drawing board. Four bookcases were made to his design by the estate carpenter (they have cupboards below with chicken-wire doors and are lined in maroon silk); five new upholstered gilt stools with carved shells were specially made to measure to sit beneath each of the five windows, their design inspired by similar pieces at Stanway House in Gloucestershire. After looking carefully at the pictures and mirrors in the room a choice was made and the rest moved to other parts of the house. Symmetry again: three pictures were hung over each fireplace where they are reflected in the two Chippendale gilt mirrors which have been placed on the opposite wall just in front of the fireplaces. Heavy pediments over the doors were removed to make way for Stefanidis mirrors (*above*). They add a humorous, light touch, often found in his work – rather in the 'jokes' tradition of Lutyens's architecture. Here the palm-wreathed mirrors look as if they are windows into the room beyond while reflecting the ceiling and the light from the chandeliers. The design was inspired by

Borromini's door surround in the Collegio di Propaganda Fide in Rome. 'It is more domesticated', Stefanidis explains, 'but retains some of its brio.'

A handsome eighteenth-century console table was moved to a more prominent position on the window-sill wall, and some existing marble tops were used to make additional side tables (*above*). In the centre of the picture on the left stands a Stefanidis drum table with a marble top; elements of the eighteenth century have been incorporated in this interesting modern piece which has a cage-like support and brass wire. It is useful as a cupboard or for books and its simple design mixes well with its august surroundings.

The picture on the left shows the saloon with its sitting islands. Each of these has a comfortable sofa, armchairs and a fur rug. At one end there is an ottoman upholstered in coral-red ribbed silk with a tasselled bullion fringe in two tones of red on its skirt, at the other a fine Stefanidis table with a scagliola top. This table, like everything else in the room, looks as if it belongs there and is in the right place. One of the islands is upholstered in different tones of red as Stefanidis believes that 'variations stop the eye from getting bored'. The other has four large armchairs in his 'Victoria' fabric (named

after a daughter of the house) – a pale blue-grey floral design which mixes well with the reds. A group of 1780 painted chairs carefully placed in pairs add to the successful combination of tones, as do the Imari vase-lamps with their pleated shades.

The ceiling has been enriched by additional plasterwork and new colours based on Adam designs from the archives in the Soane Museum. A drawing was made and the colours mixed *in situ*, because these change when seen from below. The photograph does not do justice to the vibrant clarity of the colours; swags and stars, not previously gilded, were picked out and the pale olive-coloured background changed to a rich terracotta which enhances the cove and at the same time 'lowers' the ceiling.

Two delightful *blanc-de-chine* Chinese figures (*p. 102*) remind one of the Chinese pavilion at Sans Souci in Potsdam. Sitting on their umbrella bases, they draw attention to the bouffant striped-silk festoon blinds which clothe all five windows like the bustles of ball dresses. Behind them the intricate patterned stencilled walls give a dramatic brocade effect to the room. Twenty different stencils were used to obtain this rendering of a sumptuous damask design by the Czainskis (*p. 38*).

as the focal point of the room, Stefanidis used its deliberately distressed colours as an inspiration for the fabric called 'Glen' which he created for the house. The fabric's mass of pale shadowy flowers is seen on a blue background on the simple draw curtains and tie-backs on the right; on the left, looking on to the garden, the windows' reefed-up blinds show the same flower pattern on an ochre background which gives the impression of sunlight and of the garden flowers beyond.

The previous owner of the house was a sad widower and the musty shroud of gloom – so often found in prewar houses – almost made the Glenconners not want to move in. But when Stefanidis began work his immediate aim was to bring in light and give the house a more lively, charming and amusing air; something more in keeping with the flair of its owner who, at a crucial point before the room was completed, went on a lightning shopping spree – without Stefanidis – and returned in triumph with a brightly-coloured Turkey carpet and two Edwardian button-back armchairs upholstered in kelim cuts. These he placed back to back, much to Stefanidis' satisfaction.

Respecting the nineteenth-century period of the house, which was probably remodelled in 1910, John Stefanidis retained the tall mahogany doors and woodwork and had them polished, and kept the original windows and the stained glass panels in the third sitting room. A seat fills an alcove, with a table covered in fabric just in front. The two Charles Rennie Mackintosh-style slate and marble fireplaces (only one is shown) in this room have a strong 1910 character which goes well with the family furniture, carefully placed by Stefanidis to its best advantage. A shelf at cornice height was retained for decoration and to display china. The sofa and armchairs fit comfortably amongst the many styles of the room, and the mass of pictures, family photos, *objets* and favourite 'things' inherited or collected by the owners.

The third sitting room (*right*) has a Regency gothic desk and chair inherited from the owner's great-grandfather's house, 'Glen', in Scotland. The desk furniture and the lamp are also in gothic style. The brass items are engraved with the gothic monogram of 'CT' for Sir Charles Tennant, the owner's great-grandfather. The grand crenellated Japanese bowl serves as a waste-paper basket.

An Arts and Crafts inspired house

The drawing room here is really three sitting rooms running into each other. Colin Tennant, now Lord Glenconner, Stefanidis' friend and client, is a man of eclectic taste who inherited a splendid collection of Arts and Crafts furniture to which he has added other different period items of his choice. Stefanidis worked around these props which included a magnificent William Morris carpet specially made for the owner's great grandparents in 1889 for their house 'Clouds' in Wiltshire, built for them by Philip Webb. Fixing on this remarkable piece

In the Avenue Montaigne a radical change was made by Stefanidis erecting mirrored 'walls' right round the hall. Two more mirrors cover the walls at either end of the small sitting room, giving an original bright look to a very ordinary room and adding a feeling of space. A Stefanidis sofa and two lacquered tables, one a cupboard, the other a bookcase (as a 'mirror' image the same arrangement is repeated on the other side of the room), and his ottomans were all an attempt to impose a definite 1930s style. This was carried through by adding four Chagall drawings, hung boldly facing one another left and right of the sofas, Lalique-type vases, decorative sculpture of that period and a blue and white Venetian mirror. The whole window wall, which had unsightly divisions, was unified by the use of blinds and fabric-covered screens which correct the proportions of the room. The chairs are again in 1930s style; the Stefanidis light reflected in the mirrors is unobtrusive, a plain ceramic pot with a shade. The pictures are hung from a chrome bar at cornice level so that they can be easily changed at will.

The contrasting room is on the first floor of a building in Eaton Square, where good proportions and tall windows looking out on the trees 'had to be treated with dignity', Stefanidis affirmed. With this in mind he gave the room one of his giant sofas covered in 'Varese' with silk cushions. He added a *chaise-longue* upholstered in his 'Chinese Weather' fabric which has a golden cloud motif. Balance is created by a specially designed large bookcase against one wall facing a handsome picture which takes up the whole of the wall behind the sofa. The bookcase, which also houses the stereo, and the large decorative horse picture, are the right bold size and make the room. Other additions which enhance its character are the two family busts in front of a window, a Thomas Hope chair, a round mahogany table and four chairs. Concealed doors (*see also pp. 31 and 89*) lead into the rest of the apartment, a device which makes one think that there are more rooms, or fewer, than there really are.

Contrasting rooms

Two very different drawing rooms face each other here. The one above, in Paris's sedate Avenue Montaigne, lacked character and called for major alterations. The other, on the right, is in London's dignified Eaton Square and has good proportions and architectural details which have been respected.

Belgravia drawing room

These two views are of another drawing room in Eaton Square (*see also p. 89*). Entering through its pink and grey columned hall – which is quite a surprise in London – one is drawn forward towards the light and trees framed by the drawing room's three long terrace windows. In the morning light, the colours of this room – discreet tones of white on white with a tinge of beige and yellow – have the freshness of a field of daffodils. Between the delicate unlined silk taffeta curtains, with their attached pelmets (for uninterrupted light) and knife-pleated edges, there are two Stefanidis china cabinets. Their pyramidical shape and size has been governed by the small space between the windows of this nineteenth-century room. But they serve a multitude of purposes. They give the room balance, they group together a fine collection of china which was scattered throughout the owner's previous flat, and the lighting in the cabinets throws out a glow that gives the impression that the sun is coming in from outside. As in most Stefanidis houses they are a design solution that also hides the heating.

A striking feature of this room is the mirror over the sofa. Here Stefanidis has been bold, not to say cheeky, to emulate a Grinling Gibbons mirror. The frame's solid carving and exaggerated swirls blend with his jumbo sofa and large, comfortable armchairs and the owner's antique French furniture. The placing of the mirror in this room serves the same purpose as the large picture on page 109. Since the owner did not have a picture of these proportions and did not wish to buy one, Stefanidis undauntedly constructed this de-

corative piece which is now the focal point of the room. The fabric on the sofa (also used in the Embassy in Washington, *p. 117*) is his 'Ladakh' and on the chairs his 'Jaiselmir'. The cushions are covered in Chinese silk.

A small space

At first glance this could well be the corner of a large drawing room, but it is not. It is a sitting room in a small house in Chelsea's World End with Arts and Crafts furniture, Japanese prints and a welcoming fire. The illusion is created by Stefanidis' refusal to be cowed by the small space that this conversion of a two-floored apartment presented. The drawing room now leads into the bedroom, shower and lavatory; down two steps to the kitchen and out into the garden. Below there are two bedrooms, a bathroom and kitchenette. It is John Stefanidis' mother's flat.

His answer to restricted space is to treat it boldly; this he has done with his large tall-backed sofa and armchairs covered in the two-tone colourways of his dramatic 'Chinese Weather' fabric with its swirls of clouds. A hexagonal table stands in front of the bay window-seat which hides the heating and is a favourite place to sit. The wooden fireplace has been marbelized and gas-fired 'coals' have been installed for convenience. The large mirror, though important from the de-

corative point of view, is a simple construction of reeded wood; the flowers on the mantlepiece in soldier-like line give a feeling of order and abundance and are a Stefanidis 'stamp'. There is an Arts and Crafts motif here too – an E. W. Godwin table stands by the armchair and there are William Morris chairs throughout the apartment. In the far corner there is a Stefanidis candle lamp with a painted Kashmiri shade bought flat in Srinagar and made up in London; the Bessarabian rug on the floor is one of his favourite types of carpet (*see also p. 24*). An ingenious place was found for his mother's fierce Japanese prints, which have been mounted on to screens fashioned from the existing doors that cleverly separate the sitting room from the bedroom.

Looking through to the bedroom, the bed in an alcove is upholstered at both ends and enclosed by a curtain hung all the way round. 'So much more friendly than the wall', Stefanidis explains. The window overlooking the garden has one of his inexpensive 'inventions' – a pinoleum straw blind which, because it tends to discolour, is covered in fabric. When it is down, the slats allow a textured light through

the fabric. There are ample cupboards with simple wire-mesh doors and gathered fabric behind. This apartment has an air of prettiness rather than grandeur in a very restricted space.

A platform and fireplace

This sitting room (*right*) is in the house Stefanidis built on Patmos; not one of the many he has restored, but one he built from scratch for Axel Springer. Given the plot – a terraced steep drop to a small beach – and the dimensions required for the sitting room, he drew up his plans accordingly, mixing the Cycladic island vernacular with the essential elements for the comfort and needs of his client. Fireplaces are not traditional on Patmos but, bearing in mind that the house was sometimes to be used before the summer heat, Stefanidis knew that one would be a welcome addition. The platform is a typical Greek feature also found in Northern Greece and the islands. Here it is rimmed with a wooden balustrade inspired by the design of a screen in the Indian palace of Padmanabha-puram and repeated on the staircase of the house. The room might have been dark but Stefanidis used the Patmos device of a ceiling opening which lets the light flow in from the terrace above (*see also p. 51*); this gives ample light in the daytime and there are two Angle-poise lights for reading at night. The sofas, covered in Stefanidis fabric, are immensely comfortable. A durrie in the foreground, an oak table, a lamp and a sofa provide the simple comforts of this island room where two silver-clad icons look down on the serene scene. The ceiling could have been there for centuries but the beams, which came from the island of Samos, are new. In between these Stefanidis has used bamboo which, in the past, held up the rubble filling between floors and now, although no longer necessary because of modern insulation, is nevertheless a decorative device which recalls the ancient practice. The small windows with inner shutters are traditional on the island – useful to keep the sun out in the summer and the warmth in during the winter. The terracotta-tiled floor is also true to Patmos tradition, a craft which had died out until revived by John Stefanidis. The whitewashed walls and pale green paint on the woodwork give a cool transparency to a house where the past enhances the present.

A Greek parlour

This room (*left*) is on Patmos too, but it has a different atmosphere. Once a prosperous sea captain's house in the nineteenth century, it still retains its solid respectability. When Stefanidis began work here, the house had been lived in for some years but needed rearranging and decorating. The whitewashed walls inside and out were retained and the traditional island blue paint used for the door surrounds and windows – on the shutters blue was picked out in shades of blue and grey for a more decorative effect. The kelims on the floor and the kelim cuts used to upholster the chairs on the left give the room a medley of rich colour. The chairs on the right and the sofas (not shown) covered in Stefanidis' white on white 'Mahal' fabric, a contrast to the low table's multi-coloured antique embroidered patchwork cover and the Rhodian embroidered cushions. The painted ceiling has wooden boards with joists carefully covered by blue fillets and a highly decorative blue and white and gold ceiling rose in the centre. In the foreground a collection of white opaline glass vases and jugs are massed together in Stefanidis style and at the far end of the room, through the door, you can see the dining room (*p. 128*).

A painted door

A detail (*right*) of a fine Patmos door. These doors were part of the wooden enclosure which housed the bed or mattress up to the eighteenth century. Rather like a room within a room, they first had wooden doors and walls – instead of curtains, then later half-glazed partitions. The naive motifs shown here are reminiscent of the island's early decorative art and examples are to be found in the museum of the Monastery of St John. In the stencilled rendering of such designs, Stefanidis has added the stronger motifs taken from the kelims on the floors.

Working with Stefanidis in Washington

John Stefanidis decorated the British Embassy ballroom for the 'Lutyens 1982 British Embassy Showcase' when my husband was the British Ambassador and I invited leading British designers to decorate a room in the Embassy using British fabrics. The object of the Exhibition was to show the prestigious Queen Anne style building, completed by Lutyens in 1928, brought up to date with the best of British design and taste. Former Ambassadors and their wives had left their mark and this was particularly evident in the majestic processional gallery and the ballroom. Here, what Lutyens had visualized as neoclassical order, or what he impishly called 'Wrenaissance', had been transformed into British gloom and disorder. Although the walls were flaking badly, as Lutyens was not too good on plumbing, there was one focal point in the room – a handsome Tabriz carpet designed for the opening of the Great Exhibition at the Crystal Palace by Queen Victoria in 1851.

Before John Stefanidis arrived in Washington I tried to find out what the ballroom looked like when just built; but the Foreign Office could not help, nor the PSA (Property Services Agency, now part of the Department of Environment), and dreary black-and-white photos were produced when I was interested in the colours. Help came from my Washington friends and from old Washington press cuttings; all indicating white walls, a yellow glow and a country house atmosphere. This was Stefanidis' brief. But the 'yellow glow' was originally shed by the scagliola columns and the chimneypiece surrounds and these had been painted over by one of my predecessors. When I suggested to the PSA that we strip off the paint to return to Lutyens's concept they came back with a warning: 'The paint must be hiding damage.' Lutyens also dramatically emphasized the white walls, the frieze and ceiling by placing high dark mahogany doors alternately with smoked glass mirrors in a black and white theme repeating the chequered marble and slate floor of the colonnade and reminiscent of his masterpiece, the Viceroy's House in New Delhi. But the mirrors had been replaced by general store gilt copies and the doors covered in white paint. Anxious to get started, and ignoring official advice, I scraped a little paint off the columns one night and showed them to a leading American architect who was delighted and urged me to go ahead. Since the columns were unharmed, the whole colonnade was scraped and polished, so were the chimneypieces and mahogany doors. And, thanks to a tip from one of the painters, the smoked mirrors were found in the attic, all numbered and easy to replace.

On arrival Stefanidis took one look at the furniture, which had already been plundered by the designer David Mlinaric for his sitting room and by others for their rooms too: 'Palm Court hotel stuff,' he said, eyeing the sagging Edwardian chairs and sofas and non-period tables. 'The British Embassy Ballroom *must* have some good furniture.' Happily, private donors in England came to our rescue with two George III gilt console tables and a large round centre table. These provided the necessary balance and order and, together with some pieces Stefanidis collected from other rooms, more or less satisfied 'The Master' as my staff and I referred to him. He then carefully arranged the room into separate little sitting areas, ordering a goatskin rug in front of one fireplace and an ottoman for the other. These produced a light-hearted approach, informality, comfort and ease – even if a little unusual for an Embassy ballroom. Then he insisted that he must have busts on pedestals and real candles in the chandeliers. I tried to explain that the PSA did not provide busts at will and that real candles in an official residence required an army of tall butlers with snuffers. On a trip to London, John Stefanidis and I visited the Royal Academy where, thanks to the President Sir Hugh Casson's blessing, we were handed a torch and taken to the basement store. There, stepping over marble feet, hands and busts, we drew out appropriate heads. These were shipped to Washington and set on 'scagliolized' wooden pedestals, the work of a gifted British grainer. In desperation about candles I happened to notice electrically adapted real candles in the renovated eighteenth-century Gunston Hall, Virginia, which had been admirably restored. Although made in the US they were installed in the three chandeliers by our Embassy electricians.

The ballroom's functions are multiple now. It is used as an informal drawing room, a state room for investitures and a dining room with round tables for 250. Today it is back to the way Lutyens saw it or, to be more exact, it is Stefanidis' interpretation of Lutyens's original design, as Lutyens never took much notice of the final decorative details of this commission because he resented the British Government's attempt to cut his bill and reduce his plan. The blue and white Wedgwood frieze has been painted in two tones of white and the columns and walls repainted in a similar manner. The white paint was mixed by Stefanidis on site with our painters, and each column and garland marked out so that the lighter shade covered the protruding form and the darker shade the wall behind. Ethereal, unlined, flowing double-silk curtains in peach over yellow pick up the scagliola tint and give the 'glow' that Lutyens wanted – but his curtains, following the fashion of the day, would have been skimpier and heavier. Colefax & Fowler and Stefanidis chintzes cover the re-upholstered 'hotel furniture', giving the whole room the atmosphere of a country house and bringing the sunlight and garden right into the room. 'The Master' ordered lilies for the opening. Our gardener did his best and a few lined the columned corridor – otherwise the Embassy silver wine coolers, soup tureens and all the vases in the house were packed with white, peach and yellow flowers – 'The Master's' colours.

DINING ROOMS

It is not clear when the term dining room was first used. In France, in the early eighteenth century, meals were often served in one of the antechambers – those connecting rooms leading from the bedroom to the salon where the more formal dining took place. Later the French also had food taken to their bedchambers where small occasional tables were set up. The British, however, preferred to use a dining parlour for family and close friends and a saloon or a great dining room for grand occasions. In the nineteenth century, when serving meals for a large number of guests was no longer the fashion in England, the dining parlour became the dining room with a more masculine decor and a 'closet' for gentlemen's use, replacing what had shocked the French – that chamber pot in a corner! And whereas the French at that time used their *salles à manger* – eating rooms – solely for eating and kept a simple decor as a backcloth to their ornate dishes, the British on the other hand tended to treat their dining rooms as a place to relax, linger, drink, smoke, converse and discuss, after the ladies had, of course, withdrawn. But all these mannerisms and habits usually relate to large houses and palaces, few of which exist today; yet the French still look on their dining rooms differently from their English counterparts. Though it is difficult to generalize, a Frenchman concentrates more on food than on the decor which is kept sedate; an Englishman is more interested in conversation and wine and likely to leave the decoration to his wife.

Nevertheless, many of the ideas of those early years have left their stamp today. The footstools for ladies' comfort are no longer necessary as floors are not cold and shoes not so thin. Instead there is an emphasis on comfortable chairs and Stefanidis designs his with comfort in mind. Round tables and tables with flaps and rims are still the fashion. Stefanidis

prefers round tables because they are best for conversation, less pompous, and fit the smaller-sized modern dining room. Marble-topped sideboards are back in fashion too, but not necessarily white as they usually were in the eighteenth century – Stefanidis often prefers a honey colour which is warmer and he uses it for side tables, consoles and dining tables (*p. 127*). Urns sometimes decorate his dining rooms too. These were, in the past, water-filled and used for washing glasses. And candles – real candles for chandeliers and candlesticks – are *de rigueur* for Stefanidis' dining rooms, as he borrows from the past when it suits the present.

On the following pages, each of his rooms varies according to different demands, the area allotted and the country he is working in. But they all have definite common themes – understated elegance, pleasurable comfort, careful lighting and often a focal point – a picture or a chandelier. The warm, enclosed feeling of his painted or stencilled walls is balanced by the simplicity of his furniture – his round, painted or marble tables and his slip-covered chairs with bows, his upholstered

chairs with arms or his painted chairs. In his outdoor dining rooms (*pp. 130–3*) the white-washed walls, the sky and the trailing flowers are used to their best advantage as he carefully adds his plain tables, some with marble, stone or tile tops, and his rush-seated or wooden chairs, or stone benches, with comfortable cushions: all strictly in keeping with what the local tradition demands.

Pop Art in Paris

The Place Fürstemberg, off the Rue Jacob, is only a few yards away from Delacroix's studio. It looks like a theatrical Parisian scene with its benches, globe street lights and tall plane trees. But the flat that Stefanidis worked on here in the late 1960s was in a building with no fine architectural features, in fact a former artisan's house with nothing more than the quintessential Parisian view. So he gutted it and started again. His aim was modern simplicity – no cornices, no dados, but carefully calculated space to house a collection of modern pictures. At first the owners wanted to house a collection of contemporary 'École de Paris' pictures, but Stefanidis argued that with Paris so emphatically outside there was need to create a contrast.

The painting (*opposite*) is by Roy Lichtenstein, a 1930s Art Deco motif which has been blown up. It follows the Pop Art creed of creating a work of art out of everyday objects or motifs and enhancing them, as painters in the past used everyday subjects for still lifes.

The artist Allen Jones's table is shown in the foreground (*above*). Looking through to the dining room, one sees a soft sculpture of a seated figure by Aeppli, a glass table, and Perspex chairs derived from a design by Eero Saarinen. Not shown is a bar with a basin and stereo fitted into a sheet of chrome. Stefanidis now finds that built-in systems are impractical since technology changes so rapidly.

A kimono motif

This dining room (*left*) in Belgravia has rich silk beige and brown striped curtains with attached fringed pelmets, and comfortable upholstered chairs with arms which stand round an oval terracotta-red lacquer table. This shape was the owner's choice as it seats two more than if it were round. Not shown here, but against the wall opposite the window, a Matthias Lock mirror hangs above a marble-topped sideboard also designed to hide the heating. The lacquered sideboard has a display of Chinese red plates. But it is the design on the walls that give the most dramatic effect to this small room. Stefanidis personally followed the stencilling work, which was taken from a Japanese kimono, making sure the charming fan design was carried out rhythmically so as to avoid the geometric look of a wallpaper repeat.

A painting makes the room

The dining room on the right is in Stefanidis' eighteenth-century house in Cheyne Walk as he first arranged it in 1972. The painting by Cy Twombly makes the room. Stefanidis believes strongly 'that one should not turn away from contemporary art in all its manifestations but incorporate it in one's life'. He is against 'cosiness for its own sake, the safeness of convention or the ghastly good taste which stifles creativity'.

The round table, painted to look like parchment, sits on a pink Spanish rug with an Arabic inscription; in the centre of the table is an Indonesian bowl, a container for rice and condiments used for taking offerings to a temple; the glasses, with gilt decoration, are nineteenth-century French; the boxes are Indian and the plates Wedgwood.

Fabric-covered walls

If you do not possess it – then Stefanidis will make it. The inspiration for the delicate lyre-shaped gilt bevelled mirror on the right came from Russia. A pair of these mirrors hang opposite one another on his yellow 'Benin' fabric-covered walls which enclose this little dining room overlooking Kensington Gardens. Paint would have been too hard for such a small plain room. The fabric is repeated on the slipcovers with bows on his dining chairs – an *en suite* approach which goes in and out of fashion, but here gives a unified look. There is a Persian rug on the floor, a nineteenth-century French table, and a large painting which hangs above a French-style console table by Stefanidis. The two mirrors reflect light and, together with the fine pair of Egyptian candelabra, add weight and symmetry to the room. The windows are dressed with silk curtains as a contrast to the cotton walls. Not a purist approach, Stefanidis accepts, 'but too much cotton is too informal, too much silk can seem pompous in a limited space'.

Patterned walls

Two round tables instead of one long one is something Stefanidis likes to do; here in this small London terraced house there are two small dining rooms leading into one another, so he placed a round table in both. His comfortable chairs with arms, designed to fit the area, stand round the tables which can seat eight. In this room, because it had no good proportions, Stefanidis devised a frolicking harlequin design with a distressed effect for the stencilled walls and added two of his cupboards with gathered fabric 'windows'. A Venetian mirror hangs over the painted fireplace and the full festoon blinds add richness to this witty little room.

A Tuscan farmhouse

This dining room (*left*) is a former cowshed transformed by Stefanidis when he converted a seventeenth-century Tuscan farmhouse at Poggio al Pozzo. He retained the manger, lowered the floor and covered it with large traditional Tuscan fired tiles. He kept the beams as 'being perfectly functional' but reinforced them with a steel horizontal cross beam which he matched up by enclosing it in wood. The rough plaster walls are lime-washed white – an excellent backcloth to the large abstract painting and the multi-coloured porcelain enamel plates. These contemporary elements – set side by side with the rush-seated turned chairs, the woven cloth on the table like those portrayed in fourteenth-century Siennese paintings, and the huge age-old oil jars – are

typical of Stefanidis' work as he carefully mixes the old with the new. The straight wine and water glasses are usual in Italy and give a touch of farmhouse simplicity. The storm lights protect the candles from breezes that waft through the terrace door and fill the room with the scent of lavender and clipped rosemary hedges from the garden outside.

The 1930s brought up to date

This dining room (*above*) is in a 1930s house in Kifissia, outside Athens (*see p. 92*). Respecting what was there, John Stefanidis kept the spirit of the house as he worked making drastic changes and adding new windows, furniture and decoration. The enlarged windows have sliding panes; there are straw pinoleum blinds and painted wooden shutters, no curtains. The

Greek light casts slatted patterns as it filters through the pinoleum or the shutters. There are no cornices. After the electricity was rewired throughout the house, ceiling lights were installed in specific areas such as over the staircase, but never above seats. Behind the screens there are two marble-topped serving tables well lit by a window and strong overhead lights. However, there are no overhead lights over the marble-topped dining table, to prevent glare. The imposing dining table, which can seat fourteen, was made from beige Dionysos marble and set in place after the floor, which is above the garage, was reinforced. The parquet floor has been stained a milky shade and there are no pictures on the walls, which are painted with swirls in keeping with the design of the screens. The ceiling is highly glazed to reflect colour and light.

Nineteenth-century Patmos

Patmos's merchants and sea captains would often return from their journeys with furniture, icons, wooden chests and mirrors; and the more prosperous would hang their walls with family portraits painted by itinerant artists. Some of these items, though flaking and in bad repair, have survived and Stefanidis has incorporated them into the houses he has restored. In this dining room (*left*) there is a tin Italian chandelier bought in London, a Greek 'Victorian' period sideboard and an Italian gilt mirror found locally; the naive paintings are also from the island. Keeping to Patmos tradition the walls are whitewashed and the window frames and shutters painted the traditional island blue. The scrubbed wooden floor is left unpolished with a kelim rug placed under the tables. Two round tables are less formal than one; the modern round tablecover is counterbalanced by the peasant-weave cotton underskirt from Stefanidis' Athens shop.

A winter room

This dining room (*right*), described by Stefanidis as a 'funny little room with a bread oven in the corner', is in a Patmos house used for guests. As it is only used in winter, the chairs and the gate-legged table are lined up against the wall as they might have been in the eighteenth century. The wooden chairs are typical of the Ionian islands and come from Corfu. Their squabs are covered in a peasant hand-woven check fabric from Northern Greece. The ceramic plates, with their naive olive branch design, were made in Crete, and, like all rustic pottery, chip easily. They are displayed in the traditional Greek manner – on a high shelf ringing the room. Stefanidis' idea here was that since the room was not used much it should be ready when it was wanted.

Stamped terracotta tiles, now made locally as in the past thanks to Stefanidis' insistence, cover the floor; the walls are whitewashed and a lantern sits in a rectangular recess.

Dining outside

Through the monastically plain stone doorway with its Byzantine cross, traditional to the island (*left above*), there is a view of two large oil jars – no longer used for oil but decorative in shape – mattress cushions on a bench and very steep steps leading to an upper terrace.

On the same level, to the right of the doorway, there is a small outside dining room (*left below*) beyond the typical Aegean arch. It has a trestle table, a bench, rush-seated stools and a lantern hanging on the wall. Simplicity is the note of the protected little room.

The picture on the right looks similar to the one on page 132, but here it is a dining area facing south and in a garden lined with sweet-smelling citrus trees. As it is sheltered, Stefanidis was able to punch out windows in the thick stone wall thus framing a biblical view. Millington-Drake plates and spiral Venini glasses from Venice look well on the rough stone table.

Terrace rooms

John Stefanidis' outside rooms and terraces are treated with the same care and precision as his interiors. In warm climates, he maintains, they are an extension of a house because 'you cannot ignore what is outside when you look out of a front or back window': there has to be a continuity of design.

The picture on the left is of a terrace dining room in a Patmos house Stefanidis designed, built and decorated. He also landscaped the garden. The solid, thick stone wall was built to enclose the dining area and acts as a shield against the prevailing Meltemi wind – the enemy of Mediterranean seafarers as it lashes out unexpectedly in the summer. There is a stone-topped table with a whitewashed cement base, locally made rush stools, and southern Italian plates which, though not indigenous, suit this outdoor room. The long bench follows three-quarters of the way round the terrace and has mattress cushions – now commonplace on Patmos since Stefanidis instructed the local midwife-mattressmaker in the art. The pebble floor, an example of an island craft, was laid by the local builder who also chose the design, an example of how Stefanidis encourages those working with him to be creative.

The terrace above belongs to the same house: it leads out from the sitting room and is twice its size. A spectacular view of the sea and the ships passing by is framed by deliberately oversized squat pillars which were inspired by a pair Stefanidis saw on a remote farmhouse terrace. The cane chair with its mattress cushions is a Stefanidis design. Stone steps lead down from the terrace to the garden.

BEDROOMS

A bedroom is private – or so it is today – unlike the sitting room or dining room which are on show to friends and guests. In contrast, however, Napoleon's favourite sister, Pauline Borghese, received her visitors lying on her *lit de parade* and Lady Diana Cooper was to do likewise years later. Pauline's gorgeous two-ended satin-upholstered *couchette* (as the inventory calls it) is the pride of the British Embassy in Paris, for the palace was bought by the Duke of Wellington for an Embassy in 1814 when Pauline sold it in haste with all its contents in order to follow her brother into exile. The bed, which has been slept in by several Ambassadors and their wives, is a wonderful example of the high Empire style of the *nouvelle vague* – the revolutionary Bonaparte genre – and in Pauline's time it stood on a dais, surmounted by hangings, a crown and eagle and twenty-six ostrich feathers. It is decorated with four half-naked Egypto-caryatids, four lions, lyres, serpents, garlands of vines, myrtle and laurel leaves. But history relates that at night Pauline slept in a little adjoining room on a small pink-curtained bed decorated with a few feathers. This was often a choice made in the seventeenth and eighteenth centuries when not only privacy was sought but safety too, and the small closets usually had secret getaway exits.

In the early seventeenth century, most beds in Europe had dropped or drawn curtains which made them private, enclosed and warm – these hangings were often changed in summer and winter. The usual bedchamber furniture at that time could include a dressing table with a carpet cover and an embroidered linen cloth, or *'toilette'* as it was called, to protect it; a pier-glass; and several candlesticks. Chairs were lined up against the wall and a chamber pot placed near the bed. Later in the century the beds in grand houses became more elaborate, the French setting the fashion since they used

their bedchambers as salons too. Dressing tables were sometimes covered with muslin overskirts and the chamber pot hidden in a closet or a pierced chair – *une chaise percée*. Peter Thornton's excellent historical record of the domestic interior from 1620 to 1920, *Authentic Decor*, lists over twelve different styles of beds adopted during those years – ranging from the Trianon's flying tester with its intricate hangings, cupids, mirrors and tassels, to the 1920s sofa bed. Though many stately homes in England followed the French style – hence the adoption from the French of the word bedchamber (from *chambre*) – the more traditional country houses chose the simpler four-poster bed with elaborate or plain hangings. This had the head to the wall, while the French beds – prow-ended *lits bateaux*, or slope-ended *lits à double tombeau*, or their more ornate *lits à la Polonaise* with curved posts and a small dome, and their alcove beds – were often set sideways to the wall.

Prints, paintings and early upholsterers' catalogues give a plethora of ideas to decorators

today and John Stefanidis has adopted some of these, bringing them up to date. His day-beds, couches or *chaises-longues* are simple and usually stand at the foot of his beds, his dressing tables often copy the muslin over-skirts of the past and even the embroidered cloth or *toilette*. Since few people today might want to change their summer or winter bedhangings, his are there to stay; though less elaborate, the details have been carefully worked out to create the right effect. In centrally-heated houses now, bed curtains are purely decorative and need not be drawn or let down, but nevertheless Stefanidis gives them the full length of fabric they require to hang well when let down. In hot climates his silk or cotton curtains catch the breeze. In modern rooms he has adapted what was in the 1920s the 'daring' bed-sit and designed a plain, comfortable bed and upholstered bedhead that rest happily side by side with Pop Art. His bedside tables – no longer needed for the chamber pot – house books, radio and TV, and often flowers and family photographs; good reading lights are always there too.

Edwardian Kensington

Lord Glenconner has described his wife's bedroom (*opposite*) as 'a sanctuary of sleeping beauty' and his own room below as 'a thicket'. Inspired by Lady Anne's blonde beauty, Stefanidis brought golden sunlight tones into her very feminine room. He also specially designed two fabrics bearing her names – 'Veronica', the latticed material on the bed ends, and 'Lady Anne', the bunches of roses with the lattice background which cover the walls, the curtains and her *chaise-longue*. The design was inspired by the Victorian needlework carpet. The bed, made in France twenty years ago and originally hung with muslin, is now transformed into a bouffant taffeta ballgown as the clotted-cream silk taffeta follows the upright posts in a series of bunches caught up by bows. The tester and curtains are edged with bobbles which Lady Glenconner already had. The two decorative Victorian flower pictures on the wall are wittily described by Lord Glenconner as works of 'Aunt' as opposed to works of 'Art'.

For his own room (*p. 135*) Lord Glenconner wanted shade, seclusion, darkness and a recollection of the past. Stefanidis painted the dado a dark peacock blue and stencilled a frieze with a Tudor rose motif on a blue trellis copied from the bedroom ceiling at 'Glen', the Glenconner Scottish castle. The bed, made in 1925 for Viscountess Grey, Lord Glenconner's grandmother, complete with her Edwardian crewel bedcover, is hung in simple tailored, traditional box-pleated style in a reprinted William Morris fabric: 'Christchurch'. It is in keeping with the upholstered settee for which a piece of original William Morris fabric was used – once the nursery table's undercloth. Since he had a desire to see his relations, their portraits were collected and hung on the wall round the room; pencil and charcoal drawings by John Singer Sargent, Harrington Mann, Strang and Philip Burne-Jones. The corner cupboard's panels were painted by Charles Fairfax Murray and its shelves display an unusual collection of Wemyss goblets and chalices.

1970s Modern

This is a bedroom overlooking Paris's romantic Place Fürstemberg in an apartment which Stefanidis gutted (*see also pp. 118–19*). Although today's interiors may differ in detail from those of the 1970s, when Stefanidis completed this project, there are important lessons to be learnt. These have stood him in good stead today and can help others embarking on contemporary work. This book shows that Stefanidis' minimalist approach is always present in his work: he firmly dismisses Victorian clutter or a musty Edwardian past, replacing them with clean, swept interiors and light, uncluttered backgrounds to be enriched, or not, at will.

On the floor is Cogolin matting, a delicate and beautiful covering still made by hand in the South of France. The lacquered table at mattress height was made to house stereo equipment. The two Tom Wesselmann Pop Art pictures dominate the scene and fit in well with the plain white shell of the room which Stefanidis designed. The bed was placed in the middle of the room to allow for more storage space and it is covered in finest quality suede. No curtains was the brief so shutters were added which fold back, pull-down blinds to cut out the light and hanging chrome chains that give ripples of light. All the furniture was designed for the room, including the lacquered chest with chrome inset. A small concealed door leads to the drawing room, another to the bathroom in white Formica edged in chrome.

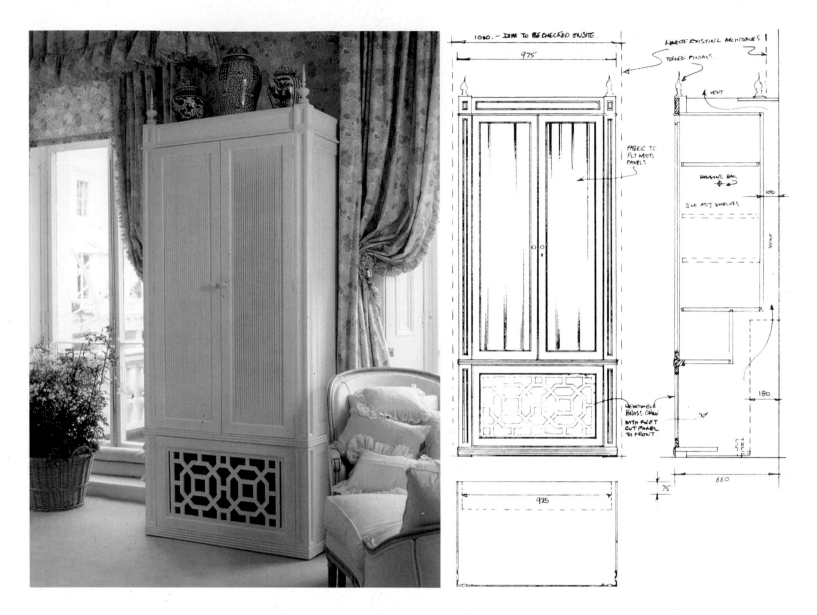

A flower-filled room

Even on a dull morning the birds are drawn to this floral bower in Eaton Square where the owner shares her breakfast with them on the balcony. Stefanidis' 'Pelargonium' fabric (designed by Millington-Drake), with its lilac, blue and white flowers, bright green crenellated leaves and Mediterranean sunbaked ochre wall background, fills the room with light and festive beauty. This is an unmistakeably feminine bedroom where the walls, curtains, sofas and buttoned ottoman, as well as the bedhead, are all in 'Pelargonium' – *en suite* in the French eighteenth-century manner. Two rooms in the apartment have been broken through to make

one. The bedroom is at one end, and in the sitting area on the other side Stefanidis has hung a Millington-Drake watercolour of a Greek interior above the fireplace which is often used. A row of *blanc-de-chine* pots stand as a *garniture* on the carved marble mantleshelf.

Since not everyone likes four-poster beds, here a high-back upholstered bedhead with two blue-grey painted turned posts was chosen. This colour has been picked up again in the three painted cupboards; two of these are large and one is small. Filling the space between the tall balcony windows, the cupboards hide the radiators set behind them; warmth comes up through carved wooden cut-out grilles based on a design by Lutyens. Their doors have

pleated fabric panels, as do the two Stefanidis bedside cupboards which add storage space. The two large lamps placed on them give good reading light. The curtains have deep pelmets with a double frill which also runs down the curtain edges. This double pinned and scalloped frill is in 'Pelargonium' on the outside, and on the inside mint green chintz which is also used for the lining of the curtains.

Throughout the room there is a subtle play of colours. The owner's *chaise-longue* (not shown) has been re-covered in pale lilac-blue silk fabric, her bergères in palest blue, her stool in a darker shade of blue and the dado painted a cantaloupe yellow – all these colours delicately merge with 'Pelargonium'.

stands of papier mâché and the dressing table mirror which stands on a covered table. The bed has a high-backed, finely pleated head-board in silk flanked by two turned wooden columns (*see also p. 139* where the same design is treated differently). The pleats on the head-board are repeated on the full valance. The bedcover looks well in the delicate quilted fabric. The curtains, in Stefanidis' 'Sultana', are French-pleated since no other treatment would have fitted the 1930s window frames of the block. A pleasant buttermilk hue now sur-rounds the bed, which was deliberately made high so that the owner could lie looking out on to the park. The light golden colour effect that Stefanidis has given this room comes from the use of different shades of the same colour – on the walls, curtains, upholstery, pleated shades and the bed. The whole design is an example of how to create a distinctive atmosphere in an uninteresting room by making a few but important changes.

Sleeping on a platform

This unexpected bedroom (*right*) is in the flat in Eaton Square described on page 108. The small space available, behind the grand, some-what conventional sitting room and through a concealed door, had to accommodate a bedroom, bathroom, sauna and kitchen. In the bedroom storage was a problem; only one cupboard could be fitted on one of the walls so a platform was made for the bed with steps leading up to it and drawers underneath. The room is tall, being on the first floor of a nineteenth-century house; to reduce the feeling of unwarranted height a low-level cornice was added and to enlarge the room visually, the windows were dressed with plain calico shut-ters and one wall was mirrored. This reflects the uncomprisingly modern bedcover in Stefa-nidis' 'Ritzy' fabric – with its bright green and peach swirls on a French mustard background. The room is an example of how Stefanidis handles a small space, and his skill in manipulat-ing height and breadth by clever design.

An Indian theme

In an apartment block facing Kensington Gar-dens, cramped space and a characterless low-ceilinged bedroom was what greeted Stefanidis when he was called in to deal with this glum flat (*above*). Light squabs were made for the owner's wooden chairs and neatly attached with bows. The Eastern design of the existing carpet was emphasized by the bold pillow and the Indonesian cushions on the window sofa which he had made to fit the alcove. These rich oriental colours enhance a collection of Indian miniatures which were hung on the wall. The Indian theme was continued with the addition of the two delicately painted Kashmiri lamp-

Two shades of white cotton

The white on white in this cool Patmos bedroom (*left*) is partly the result of the stippled doors. 'The local painters had never heard of stippling but I taught them how to do it with a broom', Stefanidis explains. The traditional handwoven Greek sheeting is another shade of white. It is used for the bed curtains – tied simply with white tape bows to the austere nineteenth-century Italian wrought-iron frame, also on the bed's underskirt below the hand-crocheted white cover, and again on the side table. The fabric has white horizontal stripes in an off-white background and its rough, uneven character is in keeping with the simple whitewashed walls and fired-tile floor.

A white china urn-shaped lamp with a plain card shade and a country mirror on the bedside table are enhanced by the bunch of blue plumbago from the garden. Blue and white are repeated on the floor in the Indian durrie. This has a flat cotton weave which Stefanidis finds cool under bare feet.

Silk and embroidery

This room in the Patmos house Stefanidis built for Axel Springer (*see also p. 113*) has several features borrowed from the ten or more houses he has restored on the island: for instance, the painted mint-green small windows and inner shutters and the whitewashed walls – though the latter display a rougher surface than the walls which are coated yearly in the older village houses. The room had more grandeur than the Patmos bedroom on the left; the nineteenth-century Italian four-poster iron bed is hung with hand-woven Greek silk in a check pattern instead of sheeting and the bed cover is a rich coloured Bokhara. The small plain painted wood-based sofa under the window has mattress cushions in the designer's style. The painted trellis table is repeated in most of Stefanidis' island houses – almost his trade mark; of the utmost simplicity, it relieves the austerity of the stone walls.

143

KITCHENS

Eating customs throughout the years have altered more dramatically than changes in design and decoration. There has been such a radical change from the time of the Roman feast of Lucullus and the later, equally extravagant banquets of sixteenth–century France when Catherine de Medici, in 1547, was served 30 peacocks, 33 pheasant, 21 swans, 9 storks, 33 turkeys, 33 flamingoes, 30 goats, 99 pigeons, 99 doves, 13 partridges, 33 geese, 13 chickens, 90 quails, 66 fowl, 90 spring chickens, 66 galantines. Meat was generally considered too ordinary, yet 40 young pigs and 100 rabbits were added as well as a galaxy of vegetables. But by the nineteenth century, although glittering and sumptuous banquets continued, both the number of guests and dishes had been greatly reduced and elegant small parties began to be the vogue. Of these Brillat-Savarin in his celebrated work on gastronomy *Physiology of Taste* says 'the number of guests must never exceed twelve, in order that the conversation shall always be general. The men should be witty, without pretensions and the women amiable, without being coquettish. The dishes should be well chosen and few in number and wine of first quality ....'

Kitchen ranges have also changed since the fifteenth and sixteenth centuries when cooking in England was often done on the hearth of a crowded hall, or later in a separate room or building where scullions scrubbed pots that had hung on chains over the hearth and cooks turned spits enveloped in smoke. Most food was either boiled or spitted, and up to the nineteenth century kitchen equipment would usually consist of an open hearth or braziers, an iron range and a wood-fired oven. By the end of the century, though, both gas and electric cookers existed even if they were only a crude version of what we have today.

Modern kitchens as we know them have rapidly gone through various stages too: mov-

ing from the clinical look to the country-style kitchen; from the fitted kitchen to one of today's favourites – the 'unfitted' look. Stefanidis offers his clients a varied choice which includes those decorated with local earthenware pots, plates and stone arches recalling the

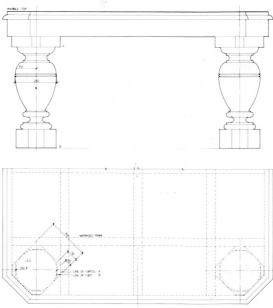

paintings of Chardin; others that go back to the hall principle with family and friends eating where food is prepared – now of course without smoke or scullions – but sometimes, as in the Italian kitchen (*left*), with a wood-fired range which the cook there uses with delight as the scent of wood envelops the meat or chicken, adding a delicious aroma and taste. In modern apartments where space is a problem, or where the owner needs all the latest equipment for preparing meals in haste, Stefanidis' pristine fitted kitchens are classical, neat and functional – everything is there and has its place to be put away tidily.

An old-fashioned table

There are three different areas in this huge country house kitchen (*opposite*): the pantry, washing-up area and cooking space. It all had to be on a very large scale; the oven large enough to cook a whole lamb and rows and rows of generous cupboards for storage. Those shown here have white opaque glass fronts. The gigantic table gives a wonderfully large working surface – every cook's dream. Designed by Stefanidis and inspired by a sixteenth-century table, it has a marble top and a bulbous solid oak base. (The scale drawing is shown on the left.) The stools are an adaptation of a Habitat design and the floor is covered in linoleum – both practical and comfortable to stand on.

A Tuscan kitchen

The kitchen (*above*) at Poggio al Pozzo, San Marcellino, in Tuscany was the only part of the once derelict seventeenth-century farmhouse that had to be newly built. Nevertheless, Stefanidis chose a traditional design to integrate it with the house. The open hearth is used for grilling – often in preference to the electric grill which has also been installed. The fireplace has an old beam above, a ledge in front for resting things on and, inset into the hood which rises straight up, there are shelves for more pots. Bunches of sweet-smelling herbs from the garden hang from hooks on the beam, to be used when grilling traditional Tuscan fare.

A brick arch divides the room and gives it the atmosphere of a peasant kitchen. (It is also reminiscent of Stefanidis' Patmos arches, *p. 130*, but those are made of stone.) In the background a simple straight-legged round table with rush-seated chairs is used for breakfast and as a working area; in the foreground there is a modern white-tiled island designed by Stefanidis. It incorporates an additional sink for washing vegetables and an excellent working surface, shown here with the traditional dappleware bowls still made in southern Italy (in green and mustard, and blue and white). In the centre there is a tiled block with sockets for electrical appliances. Not visible in the picture, but lining one wall, are the main sink, dishwasher and draining board; the cooker, cupboards, refrigerator and storage units are on the opposite wall.

Getting enough light into the kitchen was a problem because of Italy's Belle Arte rules which do not allow for the addition of extra outside windows in old buildings. Stefanidis' solution was to use a scattering of glass tiles together with the traditional terracotta ones on the new kitchen roof, to which the fan-tailed white doves who coo above show no objection.

Dorset cowsheds

Dining in a cowshed, either in Tuscany or in Stefanidis' own Dorset Cock Crow Farm (*right*), can be both rustic and formal. After looking for a country house for over three years – only liking houses 'that were too large and which made chilblains seem inevitable' – he finally snapped up a group of cowsheds with a fabulous view. These he came across when on a country walk with friends who lived nearby. Linking up the derelict buildings, he formed a U-shaped ground-floor structure which he divided into living areas. The two wings house the main bedrooms, guest bedrooms, a spacious sitting room, a studio and gallery. The kitchen-dining room joins up the two wings and is also a passage which is why it has an open-plan design. In the foreground, the table is laid with a rough cotton tablecloth from Italy – a traditional weave. The plates were specially made for the house.

The raised fireplace on the right is used, as in Tuscany, for added warmth and for grilling with a rotating spit on the open hearth. The kitchen ceiling was originally the hay loft's floor as can be seen from the cut in the beam. The idea of ceilings at different heights is a Stefanidis ploy which he has often used to break up visually the volume of a room and to alter proportions (*see also p. 96*). Walls were built out to accommodate a refrigerator and a double oven. There is a practical island unit with a scrubbed wooden top and stools around it. The tiles on the wall are the same as those on the floor and easier to keep clean than the brick in the dining area. The figure in the background is Stefanidis' cook and minder Mr Aubry. The two chairs on the left are a Stefanidis design and are covered in pink 'Scritch Scratch'; for extra comfort they are bigger and bulkier than his usual spoon-back chairs. The radiator cover on the left is used as a sideboard, its design recalling the original cowshed slats.

John Stefanidis believes that houses should not be static and looking at this picture, taken some time ago, he has noted the changes. Two cupboards have been added on the left and right of the cooking area. The one on the right is heated for drying towels, the one on the left for china. The decorative plates on the shelves are no longer there and their place is taken by 'an eccentric painted tower which is a grandfather clock'. A multi-coloured cotton durrie now covers the tiled floor. Specially made for the room in India, it was chosen by Stefanidis because, as he explains, 'I like the flat weave; it is also cheap and washable, essential in a climate where shoes are often muddy.'

There is no folksy old-world treatment in this country kitchen; instead there is bare simplicity and practicality which adds to the sparse elegance of the design. The garden 'rooms' just outside are clipped and carefully pruned with similar severity.

Keeping to the rules

In his Patmos houses Stefanidis does not impose his art, instead he has revived ancient techniques and customs. And when he has completed a project nothing jars. This Patmos kitchen (*left*) had two ovens but both had collapsed. Instead of starting anew, Stefanidis rebuilt one, which can be seen on the left of the picture, and behind it he arranged the sink. The jutting-out wall, with its top of terracotta floor tiles, is a working area as well as a 'back' for the dishwasher. The old island shelves Stefanidis finds impractical but pretty and traditional to Patmos. The plates from the island of Samos and the old rush-seated chairs were bought locally. Also traditional is the cage-like structure hanging from the beams which is a larder for cheese and fruit. The decorative circular Turkish tray – a Greek *kafenion* favourite – which is held by the ring and swings dangerously, has been painted blue. Whitewashed walls, exposed beams, a terracotta-tiled floor and a deep, small window are all in a vernacular which the designer has respected.

A country kitchen

Kitchens, Stefanidis decrees, must be functional and tidy. 'Kitchens', his client added, 'must be friendly and this one is also a breakfast room.' The result shown here (*right*) is a successful combination. The plain curtain treatment   the pole and striped fabric – was Stefanidis' idea and he designed the round breakfast table and the general plan of the room. The country pine chest on legs was found by his client, as were the chairs. She wanted a wooden floor – nothing clinical – so this is what Stefanidis gave her. Suitable commercial units were chosen and above these, to make them look more decorative, there are open display shelves. Although not shown here, the cooking area also includes a door leading to a larder with a heated rail for drying towels. None of this paraphernalia must be seen in Stefanidis' neat kitchens! There is discipline throughout even if at first glance the room just looks like a

farmhouse kitchen. Careful lighting has been installed; ceiling lights and plain wall bulkhead lamps add, or often make up for the lack of sunlight from the french window. The kitchen in this eighteenth-century house looks as if that has always been its purpose – but of course now brought up to date.

island, but here it is large enough to be used as a table to sit at on jolly green 1970s tractor stools – more comfortable than they look. Again, like the Italian kitchen, the island incorporates a small sink for washing vegetables, a chopping board and a raised tiled block with sockets for electrical equipment.

The cooking area in the background contains efficient modern appliances; to the left a refrigerator; in the centre, and well lit by the skylight above and the reflection of the strong light on the white-tiled wall, there is a sink; and to the right a double oven. The hob on the right has open space below for pots and pans and above a ledge for salt, flour and other containers. No other food is stored in this ultra-tidy kitchen except that which is kept in the refrigerator – the rest is housed in the adjoining larder. The floor is covered with non-slip grey tiles; the light from above and from the windows is not only a delight for a cook but is equally enjoyed by Stefanidis' plants in the window and on his white-tiled table. This room has been aptly described as 'a cross between a hospital and a greenhouse', but the severity is brightened by the green tractor stools and the potted plants – not to mention the delicious food served from what Stefanidis calls his 'utilitarian kitchen'.

Slick and functional

A sharp contrast to Stefanidis' hooded brick ovens and rustic hearths is this narrow, highly functional kitchen which resembles an efficient ship's galley (*right*). Here he has disposed well-constructed commercial units and added a 1930s stool designed by Louis Sognot. The floor covering is practical linoleum and the plain striped roman blind is in keeping with the clinical look. The kitchen has been carefully planned for maximum efficiency in a small area. The washing machine and dryer on the left are stacked to take up less room, and on the same side there is a sink and working top. On the right the cooking area has a ceramic hob, ovens and a refrigerator.

A former billiard room

This kitchen was once the dark panelled billiard room in Stefanidis' former nineteenth-century house in Chester Square. Ripping off the interior panelling he replaced it with pale

grey clinical tiles. The ornate plaster cornice in Edwardian Renaissance style, with its masks and garlands, was kept and painted flat white – only the centre was cut out to make room for a huge rectangular skylight. As in the Tuscan kitchen (*p. 145*) there is a central white-tiled

BATHROOMS

Tented bathtubs lined with cloth, ladies bathing in their chemises, water closets without water – just chairs with a circular hole cut out of the seat and a basin below to be emptied by servants, known in France as a *chaise percée* – these are but a few of the seventeenth-century precursors of the bathrooms and bathing practices we know today.

By the eighteenth century some grand houses might have boasted the inclusion of a bathroom with a lavatory; the latter are referred to in France as the *lieux à l'anglaise* and are said to have been invented by the British. These *lieux* or 'loos' were, however, quite rare in England although the Duke of Devonshire at Chatsworth is said to have installed ten water closets by the late 1700s. Far more common were the bathtub in tinned copper or wood often brought into the bedroom, the free-standing bath, or the canopied bath in a niche. At this time tents or curtains created the effect of a Turkish bath, and in addition there was usually a couch for an after-bath rest. It was the Americans in the late nineteenth century who began building their bedrooms and bathrooms *en suite*, so leading the way to the arrangement we now take for granted.

Though John Stefanidis' bathrooms vary in decoration, all have one important feature in common – they are luxurious. Whether in a great house or in the restricted space of a small apartment, or an island shower room, the towels are warm and usually hang on giant heated towel rails, the light is always good, and, as Stefanidis finds that people have very definite ideas about bathroom floors, these are always adapted to the individual's taste – marble slabs, fired tiles or a soft rug. The walls are carefully mirrored, cool whitewash for a summer house or tiled and marbelized for a more sophisticated town or country house or apartment.

Veined marble

In the one-bedroom apartment overlooking the Thames in Chelsea (*see also pp. 30–5*) the walls of this small bathroom are covered with warm sepia veined marble which glitters in the bright overhead light. Inset lights in the wall cupboards, to the left and right of the hand-basin, balance the ceiling lights and give a good light by which to make up or shave. The tall heated ladder towel rails, the buttoned stool and the marble step from the carpeted floor to the bath add comfort to this luxurious small golden room.

Greek island bathrooms

Stefanidis' Patmos bathrooms – with their local stamped terracotta tiles and whitewashed stone walls – are cool and chaste for they are used mainly during the hot summer months. The furnishings are sparse in keeping with the monastic simplicity of the island's architecture, but everything essential is there from well placed lighting to showers and WCs. Some (*right*) are decorated with mint green trellised cupboard doors beneath the handbasin. Others have brilliant cobalt blue-painted cupboards and mirrors copied from local designs (*left*).

The arched bathroom (*below right*) was once a kitchen, and a basin has been installed on the former 'washing up' ledge by the window. A cotton kelim is laid on the floor and there is a plain island sofa with mattress cushions. The recesses beyond the arch, where once pots and pans stood and bread was baked, are now used for decoration, displaying island ornaments such as a pewter jug and basin – a reminder of when there was no running water.

Black granite

The master bathroom of this Norman Shaw country house (*left*) was created by dividing an existing bathroom in two to give a separate dressing room which incorporates the original period window.

Complicated plumbing is concealed beneath the step leading into the marble-floored bathroom where the white-plastered walls have been perforated with recesses to house the bathroom fittings. Each of these is lined from floor to ceiling with black granite slabs with a matt, honed double border just below cornice level. The axis of the window has been respected and emphasized by the major recess facing it which encloses the bath with its black granite surround and clear glass shower screen (this folds right back when not in use). To the left of the bath there is a tall ladder towel rail and a handbasin; the WC and bidet on either side of the large opening to the dressing room are also set into recesses. The granite was chosen here to increase the feeling of depth and to contrast with the white-plastered walls; the bold use of black and white instills order and discipline.

Standard white tiles

This white-tiled bathroom (*right*) is a guest bathroom in the same turn-of-the-century house as the dramatic bathroom shown opposite. The guest bedroom has a dressing room off it which leads to the bathroom shown here. Once again Stefanidis' plan is designed around the existing period window. Adjacent sliding doors, concealed within the thickness of the walls, allow the WC and bidet to be closed off from the bathroom proper. On one side of the bathroom is a marble-topped vanitory unit below a mirrored cupboard; its two outer doors open up to reveal adjustable glass shelves, while the centre is a light box which allows light to be emitted through a sandblasted border around the mirror. On the other side, the bath is situated in a similar recess, and two large heated towel rails set in tiled recesses flank the opening to the dressing room. The entire room, including the floor, is tiled, care having been taken with the measurements to avoid any cutting. A chequered tiled frieze runs around the room just below the cornice. The standard white tiles do not prevent the bathroom from being luxurious. The highly ordered arrangement of the tiles, walls and fittings creates an atmosphere of calm.

A room with a bath

This is not a clinically tiled or dramatic granite bathroom (*left*). Instead it is a room with a bath, table, family photographs and a needle-point rug. Drawings of children line the walls and a collection of shells is displayed on the bath shelf. Overhead light comes from a pendant lamp which can be pulled up or down over the dressing table; a framed mirror over the basin has bracket lights on either side. In this room marble has been used most sparingly – merely as a decorative inset on the panelling.

Elmwood bath top for the vicarage

The design for this bathroom (*right*) in a rambling Victorian vicarage was influenced by the surrounding wooded countryside. The bath has a generous elmwood top – reminiscent of a Victorian butler's pantry drainer – and around the corner, but not shown, is a hand-basin also with an elm top. The floorboards are elmwood and the bath surround and walls to dado height are tongue and grooved wooden slats. A heated ladder towel rail and a large white tiled shower with a chrome and glass door are unmistakeably modern functional features. The outer shower walls are tongue and grooved wooden slats which stop below the ceiling to avoid the tight feeling of an enclosed space. 'Country bathrooms should have windows,' Stefanidis asserts, and here light comes from the window, from ceiling lights and a light fitting over the handbasin. The white painted walls and wooden slats brighten this small country bathroom where wood adds warmth of texture and colour.

PHOTOGRAPHIC ACKNOWLEDGEMENTS

The authors and publishers would like to thank the following photographers and magazines for their help in supplying illustrations and for permission to reproduce them:

Michael Boys: pp. 6, 91, 150
Pascal Hinous: pp. 92, 96, 108, 118, 119, 126, 127, 137, 145
A. Eisedal: p. 90
David Montgomery: pp. 2, 36–47, 98, 102–5, 122–3, 144, 149
Derry Moore: pp. 93, 116–17, 158
James Mortimer: pp. 16–29, 64–7
Karen Radkai: pp. 68–79
Fritz von der Schulenburg: p. 12
John Vaughan: pp. 10, 11, 94–5, 97
Architectural Digest (photographs by Derry Moore): pp. 100, 115, 128–9, 130–1, 142, 148

Architectural Digest (photographs by James Mortimer): pp. 80–5
Harpers & Queen (photographs by Michael Williams): 109, 141
Courtesy *House & Garden*. Copyright © 1986 by The Condé Nast Publications Inc. (photographs by David Montgomery): pp. 88–9, 110–11, 120, 138, 139, 140
Vogue (photographs by James Mortimer): pp. 121, 146–7
Vogue (photographs by David Montgomery): pp. 144, 156, 157
The World of Interiors (photographs by David Montgomery): pp. 106, 107, 134, 135, 157, 159
The World of Interiors (photographs by James Mortimer): pp. 30–5, 48–63, 112, 113, 114, 132, 133, 143, 151, 152–3, 155